DOG GROOMING
AN OWNER'S HANDBOOK

DOG GROOMING

AN OWNER'S HANDBOOK

AGNES MURPHY

THE CROWOOD PRESS

Contents

Introduction

Congratulations on taking the plunge to learn more about looking after your dog's coat and health through the guidance of this book. It is creditable of you to be concerned enough, after buying your pet, to want to look after it as well as you can. A lot of bonding occurs, through touch and voice stimulation, when an owner grooms their own dog. This can reassure the animal, or even result in the dog showing more respect to the owner by allowing them to handle the whole of its body and not just areas of which it approves.

The purpose of this book is to help owners who are struggling to maintain their pet in between going to the groomers for a professional trim, or to enable them to complete a basic trim on their own dog. If it is a breed that requires more elaborate styling then more tuition may be necessary to master this to a higher level; however, being able to groom out a dog and to keep it knot free is essential and beneficial, not just for the dog but for the satisfaction of the owner, as it enables the dog to be styled in the manner they prefer.

Often groomers are met with matted dogs and this is often a bone of contention between the owner and the groomer, as the owner usually wants a longer trim. The groomer has the welfare of the animal to consider before style so, as you will see shortly, for various reasons, the expectations of the owner are only possible if the dog is on a regular schedule with the groomer or if the owner becomes competent in maintaining their dog themselves.

The Animal Health and Welfare (Scotland) Act 2006 states that animals must not be put through pain for any procedure including de-matting during grooming. This, rather than looks, should be the goal of any pet owner. The only way to allow a groomer to do a good job on the animal, or for you, yourself, to achieve a good groom, is to present the dog knot free so that they (or you) can spend the time on the styling and the finish of the dog. It is not practical, ethical or legal to spend hours de-matting a dog before cutting it. You may, as an owner, be unclear as to why you are being asked to bring your dog on a schedule to the groomer that seems excessive. The dog can only tolerate a certain amount of time being groomed in one session and also the time spent standing is limited, again, to what is fair on the dog on welfare grounds.

If your dog happens to be one of a more labour-intensive trim or coat type, it is essential that it is groomed regularly and kept in shape to avoid the grooming process from becoming a lengthy one. The other factor that affects finish, style and duration of the trim is the temperament of the dog. If a dog is reluctant to let you brush or handle its feet or face, for example, it is at a higher risk of injury, especially when it comes to the scissoring stage. It is therefore very important that owners train their dog to be groomed right from the puppy stage. It is not the groomer's job to train them for you but, with a competent groomer, the dog can get better with the procedure as time goes on as long as an owner follows training suggestions given to work on at home.

Many owners arrive at a grooming salon and say that their dog will not let them brush it so, as you will understand, it is very difficult for anyone to do anything with this kind of dog either, unless the owner practises lessons at home in between grooming visits and understands that a perfect groom is probably not going to be achievable initially. Often, puppies will bite when you hold their face to begin with but it is vital that they are trained to allow this to be done by kindness and reward so that they do not receive any injuries, especially around the eyes, ears or mouth when cutting the face.

Initially, owners should take advantage of groomers who offer puppy taster days, after all vaccinations have been done, to get the puppy used to being handled by a stranger and all the noises associated with a salon. This can include a puppy spa bath and manicure. This should make it easier for you in the long run if you decide to groom the dog by yourself. So, as you see, there is a lot more to grooming than cutting the dog, and its success is often attributed to the work done behind the scenes by a good owner. This book may also give owners the very basic skills on which to practise before possibly deciding on dog grooming as a career. It can often show how precise the process can be and also how awkward many dogs are when being handled if they are not taught to accept grooming from a puppy or by retraining at a later stage.

One advantage of the book is that home groomers and students are made aware of the grooming equipment available and the use of tools prior to starting their grooming project. As owner of a grooming school, I know it takes a little time for a student to be aware of the types of tools and how to use them at the beginning of a course, and it can be very confusing for someone who has never groomed before. If you have learned the basics before you start you will progress more quickly at the beginning, thus giving you more time to concentrate on the grooming processes and styling.

This book is a 'go-to' for any owner wishing to learn basic grooming for their own dog or to learn, through practice, to keep their dog in a practical, easy shape for their lifestyle and capabilities. This book will not include the more advanced or complicated styles that need to have many years of training to do well but will help the owner save money on professional grooming to some extent. With some patience and practice, the pet owner can keep their animal in a tidy, acceptable manner that will improve the health and well-being of their pet through more regular grooming and care. The book will also help the pet owner understand the procedures in the grooming process and, through basic health checks, enable owners to pick up problems that, if left, may result in the dog becoming severely ill. Common parasites may be identified and steps can be taken to eradicate them before it becomes a huge infestation when they become more difficult to get under control. This is important to pet owners who may have children or other animals in their home.

The benefits of grooming are massive if done regularly and you will have much pleasure in seeing your dog looking clean, smart, well groomed and pest free at all times. Adjustments can be made and styles adapted as you please without having to wait for your next grooming appointment; if your dog rolls in something nasty like fox poo or needs to have its coat shortened quickly, you will therefore have most of the skills needed to do a reasonable job. Professional dog grooming is a highly skilled profession that takes years to do competently to a high standard. Never take your groomer for granted as they will have spent a large amount of money and time perfecting the correct way of grooming many breeds with the subsequent styling to match.

You are probably unlikely to be going to achieve the high standards of a qualified groomer quickly through this book alone, but you can certainly keep a clean, healthy and smartly groomed pet dog by getting help from this publication along with a little practice.

Good luck on your journey.

CHAPTER 1

Welfare and Safety

There are not many groomers who do not have animal welfare at heart. The Animal Welfare Act UK 2006 states that animals should not experience pain and suffering but, unfortunately, this is what often happens when an owner attempts to remove lots of knots or more severe matting out of a coat. The mats are also usually situated on the more delicate areas of the body, for example the groin, under the armpits, between the back legs, the ears and so on. These parts are more painful for the dog to have pulled or brushed and are also more prone to skin damage, so you can understand why the poor animal then begins to jump about or resents grooming long term. Most groomers are taught how to remove small knots and occasional mats with minimal suffering to the dog; however, in lots of cases, they are too far gone to proceed without the animal suffering pain.

Owners find it difficult to comprehend why a groomer cannot leave some hair on a matted dog and why the groomer often has to shave the dog to a shorter length. If the hair is cut above the mat, the mat will still be left. If the mat is cut through its thickness, not only will some still be left but you will blunt your blades. The correct placement of the blade is to point it downwards underneath the mat. Looking at the small gap between the mat and skin, you will have to cut shorter than what you would probably be happy with. If you look at the photograph, you will see where the mats lie in the coat and where the clipper has to be placed to remove them successfully. People sometimes say here is no gap at the root but this is not the case as it does not come out of the skin matted.

This shows how important it is to get to the root of the trouble.

OPPOSITE: An Italian Gundog is a multitasker. He hunts, points and retrieves.

Legs are an area that cannot sometimes be successfully de-matted without distress to the dog and this results in a clip that is smooth all over. Because these areas are not ones that the dog easily tolerates, the owner usually only brushes and combs the back of the dog and then leaves the awkward parts. This results in those parts getting worse so, when the time comes for the dog to eventually be groomed, these areas are unable to be saved without discomfort to the animal. There is no point in having a perfectly groomed body if the legs are still matted, as you cannot clip off the legs and leave the body without the groom looking ridiculous and unbalanced.

On some occasions, if some mats can be clipped out and do not affect the overall style of the groom too much, and the longer body hair hides the shorter area, a shape may be able to be achieved. A good compromise can be to shave off the undercarriage totally, along with the armpits, and leave the hair on the sides to conceal the parts of the body that cause problems to the owner and dog when grooming.

Another problem that can result in a dog having to be shaved off is when the owner continually baths their pet or allows it to get wet, especially if it has a wool or wool-cross coat. A wool coat cannot be allowed to get wet and dry on its own or rubbed with a towel without it becoming matted quickly. Imagine the scenario of putting wool into hot water and leaving it. It will become felted. This is what happens with these coats unless they are thoroughly dried with a hairdryer, slicker brush (*see* Chapter 2) and comb right to the skin as it dries. Even Cocker Spaniels' feathering becomes a problem if the dog is allowed to go swimming, for example, and not dried in the aforementioned manner.

There is a line beyond which professional work is usually required when the job is out of the realms of a pet owner. This happens when the dog is exceptionally matted and the whole coat comes off like a fleece. This has various very tightly bound sections that are not safe for an inexperienced person to attempt. There is a great risk of cutting the dog if, because the owner is unskilled in using clippers, they decide to try to use scissors to cut out the mats. Either they will cut on top of the mats, leaving them in place with just the ends of the coat removed, or they will try to go under them, cutting the skin instead. I have lost count of the number of times owners have phoned me to fix their dog as they have attempted to cut it themselves and cut the dog instead. This usually happens as they do not want the whole coat off but realize, after their attempt, that it is not as easy as they first assumed.

The answer is to maintain the coat correctly between grooms or keep the dog in a manageable style that also suits the lifestyle of the family. Unless you want to be religious in attending the groomer or grooming by yourself every few weeks for the whole of the dog's life, a short style may be the best answer for most busy families. You will need to invest in good-quality equipment and spend some of your free time keeping the dog free of mats and tangles after almost every outing.

I am no different from other groomers who have had clients say that their dog has no knots when, actually, as the comb is taken through the coat, it sticks at the hair next to the skin and will not slide through easily. What pet owners usually do then is take the comb out and put it above the knot on the outer part of the coat that has no knots. If your comb jams in the coat, that knot needs to be thoroughly teased out or it will get thicker and less manageable and become a solid mat. The last thing a good groomer wants to do is continually shave a dog's coat off. They are basically artists and want to produce a beautifully styled dog that they, and others, can admire and where the owner is pleased with the result. Ultimately, however, the onus is on the owner to look after the coat in between professional grooms. Revealing some of the mysteries of how professional groomers deal with different coats and try to solve grooming problems, this book will help you become proficient in keeping your dog looking good.

Puppy Grooming

It is really important to introduce a puppy gradually to the grooming process. Owners often make the big mistake of not taking their puppy to be groomed by a professional early enough. This is an area where it may be better to have your puppy started by someone who knows how to handle puppies and get them used to strange sounds and procedures, as you, through inexperience, may cause your puppy to either avoid or be afraid of the grooming process. This is particularly true when it is necessary to use clippers or scissors as one wrong move and the puppy could be badly injured. Well-trained groomers will be happy to work with owners to avoid a bad start to the puppy's experience of the grooming process. It will be much easier for you to work with a steady dog on the table than one who will not let you complete any work on it because it is jumping about or biting and is resistant to being groomed.

It is very important for an owner to bond with their dog during their grooming sessions.

When you are grooming your puppy, keep the sessions relatively short but never finish when the puppy is being naughty – always try to finish on a positive note. To begin with, do plenty of work in handling the dog and getting it used to being brushed and combed from the start, with gentle strokes with your hand. One problem when an owner starts to groom their puppy is that they feel they want to use a gentle brush, like one for a baby for instance. This is great to get them used to having something run across their body, face and legs; however, if used constantly on its own on a coated dog, it will not be long before the coat becomes matted, as the bristles will not be going through and separating the hair.

As a groomer, I feel sorry for new owners who tell me they have been brushing their puppy faithfully and the outer hair looks fine, but when a comb is introduced it is solidly felted at the skin. This is also a problem due to coated breeds being bathed and not dried properly. Many of the wool coats or mixes will felt, just like putting wool into hot water, if they are not 'fluff dried' (*see* the 'Wool Coats' section in Chapter 2) efficiently every time they get wet. This is where guidance early on from a groomer is invaluable so that they can advise you which tools are suitable and how to use them correctly in between puppy sessions.

As suggested before, keep your lessons with your puppy at home short to begin with; then gradually increase them as your puppy grows. There is a lot that pet owners can do to help the puppy become accustomed to grooming in tandem with a competent professional groomer. Getting your puppy used to having its feet handled is one of the best lessons to practise first. Most dogs do not like this but, obviously, it is necessary if you are going to be using scissors or clippers on them at a later stage. Gently pick up your puppy's foot and reward them whenever they let you hold it without pulling it away. Increase the amount of time they are allowing you to do this; then begin to rub the foot gently all over including under the pads, finishing with a reward when they complete the lesson successfully. Teaching your dog to respond to the command 'stand' is very useful as it prevents you from having to keep lifting the dog up while grooming. Many dogs are taught to sit only and this can make grooming very difficult so, ideally, both commands should be taught.

Cutting the face is dangerous in an untrained dog, especially if it is large and strong, although small dogs do tend to have more fiddly areas where more damage could be done. Early training is the ultimate secret to successful grooming. When you begin to train your puppy, or indeed groom any dog, it is very important that the animal is safely secured or held by an assistant to avoid having an accident that may put it off for good.

If you cannot buy a suitable table to begin with, try to find a steady table that is of a suitable height for you, as bending over constantly will certainly result in a back problem for yourself. If you can position your table in a corner, this will help to secure at least the back and one side of the table and prevent the dog from falling off and causing injury. Dogs are often only too willing to escape off the grooming table at any time they see an opportunity. If a proper control system is not available right away, some kind of restraint is needed on the back wall that you

The result of using the bristle brush looks lovely but it is just scraping the surface.

can attach a neck strap to so that you are not chasing the dog all over the table. It also helps if your dog is prone to having an occasional nip at you.

A rubber mat should also be placed on the table surface to prevent the dog from slipping if you do not have a proper table with a rubber surface. A towel will not be of any use as it will slide around and often this will frighten the dog, but if you can make use of a family member or friend to begin with, they can talk gently to the dog to keep it calm or steady so that your job becomes a little easier. This method might be needed when training a puppy or with an old dog who needs reassurance. Always reward them with voice or treat when they are being cooperative.

It is worthwhile investing in a proper table and control system eventually if you are serious about grooming your own dog, as it will make grooming so much easier for you. Tables come in various forms: electric, hydraulic or portable. Obviously the electric is the most convenient if your budget allows but there are others at the other end of the market that are much cheaper. Just make sure your table is really stable. It is really important that they are used correctly to avoid injury. This should help you

be in control and make your home grooming enjoyable and successful.

Safety

When beginning to groom your dog, there are certain points that really need to be adhered to for the safety of all concerned. The one big concern, apart from cutting the dog, is giving your dog 'brush burn'. This is the scraping of the dog's skin when using a slicker brush because the brush is either too stiff for the type of coat or you are leaning or pressing too hard on one area of the body or legs when brushing. Thicker coats need a stiffer type of bristle or they will not be groomed through to the under layers; however, when using one, ensure you are not scratching the skin by being too heavy handed. Finer coats require a softer type of slicker that is much more flexible to work with. Sometimes, on the back of some dogs such as Setters, a comb is a better idea as the coat is not usually that thick at all and it also helps to lay the coat in the correct direction when drying. You can then use a slicker brush on the feathering to remove knots.

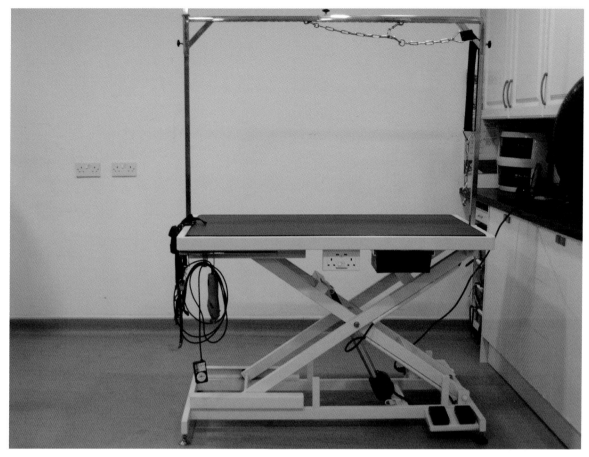

A top of the range, electric table that can be adjusted by a foot pedal. No more sore backs now.

Brush burn causes the skin to become bright red and weepy. If this happens, treat it immediately by initially putting a clean cloth on it with cold water to take the heat out of it. It may calm down at this point but, if it continues to look irritated, you may need to get an anti-biotic from the vet in case any bacteria has invaded the thickness of the skin. There may be a little blood seeping out of the area, and the cold, clean, wet cloth can help stop the bleeding. Now, some of you might feel apprehensive about this, but this does not happen often; how-ever, you need to be aware of it when brushing your pet. The answer is not to resort to a bristle brush as this will only glide over the hairs and will definitely not remove knots and tangles efficiently. Just be aware when brush-ing and avoid getting distracted by someone chatting to you when brushing your dog.

Around the face and eyes of a dog can be tricky to avoid cuts or nicks but, really, the only way to avoid this is by training your dog to have the face held. I have often had students who do not want to hold a dog in place and allow it to pull their hands off the beard or cheek that they are holding; very soon, however, they realize that it is impossible to try to use scissors around this area without keeping the dog still. As mentioned previously, early training of your pet is invaluable if you are going to attempt to groom your own dog. Practise holding its chin regularly and rewarding it only when it allows you to do it without struggling. Keep this time short to begin with until you can hold it continually. Some breeds, such as Terriers, can be particularly difficult to do this with in the early stages so, obviously, the sooner the training begins here the easier it will be for you.

Touching ears and handling feet and paws, as said before, is another good exercise to practise from the time you get your puppy. This, and with general brushing, is when we get owners saying the dog will not let them brush

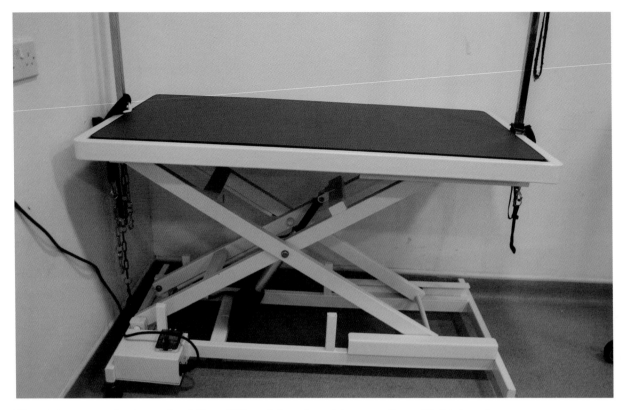

There is less worry about your dog falling off if you take extra safety precautions with this layout.

or touch it on the feet or legs, resulting in the need to shave the dog off eventually. The trick is to practise regularly, and as soon as you get your dog to cooperate, reward them with a treat or your voice. Never reward bad behaviour.

Safety on the table is important as you do not want an accident where your dog becomes injured. Always have a rubber mat on the surface of your table. A yoga mat is quite cheap and can be used successfully. This prevents your dog becoming nervous because it is sliding around on the table and is unsure of its footing. If you have any kind of table, try to position it so that it has a wall on at least two sides. This can help with dogs who are scrambling to get off or, perhaps, with an old, frail dog to help them feel more secure and be able to lie down if necessary.

A restraint should always be used, even if your dog is happy to stand on the table, as the dog can often hang its head over its feet when you are trying to see what you are doing. If you are using a neck strap, the dog is encouraged to stand straight so that you can see the shape of the leg or head that you are grooming. These restraints must be correctly used and not too tightly adjusted as this can damage the dog's internal organs. Belly straps must never be used to pull the dog up into a standing position with the strap really tight around the middle of the dog. They should only be used for preventing the dog side-stepping off the table. Three or four fingers should be able to be inserted comfortably between the abdomen and the strap. Contrary to this, if the strap is too loose, it will not serve its purpose and the dog will just step out of it. The neck strap is equally, if not more important than the belly strap.

A neck strap with a slider can be used with a thickness appropriate to the type of dog. Obviously you do not want to use a really fine strap on a Golden Retriever, for example, nor a thick one on a Yorkshire Terrier. Never have the neck strap tightly adjusted with no gap between the strap and the neck. It should fit comfortably for the dog and not be able to slip over the dog's head if it pulls back. This strap is helpful if you have a dog that doesn't like its feet being handled as, often, they can have a nip at

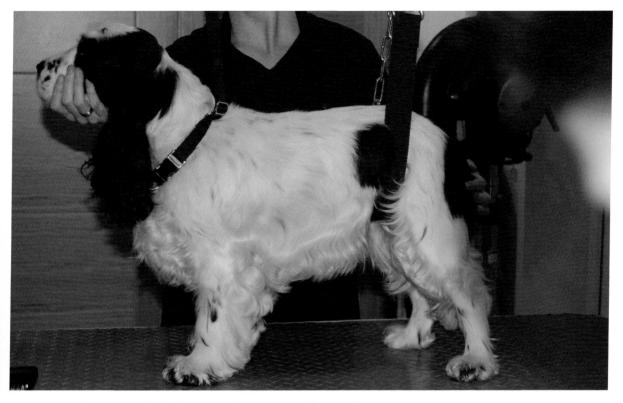

Correctly adjusted neck and belly straps will give you peace of mind when grooming.

you but you can now keep safely out of the way as the dog is restrained and cannot get right round to you.

Restraints, when used correctly, can also prevent the dog from falling from the grooming table, which could have a disastrous ending with a broken back or leg. Try to invest in good-quality restraints rather than make up your own. I have seen people wrapping chains around a control arm with the lead loose enough to allow the dog to jump but not long enough for it to allow the dog to land on the floor. This, of course, is a hanging or broken neck waiting to happen. Be safe and confident knowing that your dog is not going to come to any harm on the table by following the advice given above. One very important piece of advice that cannot be emphasized enough is *never* walk away from your dog when it is on a table.

Safety is important for yourself too as you will be working with water and electricity at times. Try to make sure you wear rubber-soled shoes and a waterproof apron when bathing your pet to prevent you slipping or getting electrocuted and to protect your clothes. You can get very itchy from the cut hair that comes off your dog, as dog hair seems to penetrate everything, and your clothes can get really spoiled by hair embedding in the fibres. A grooming tunic is ideal to prevent this. It is a good idea to use barrier cream on your hands when bathing your dog as well as it will protect your skin from the detergents and continuous dampness that can cause cracks to form. Barrier cream will also help to protect your skin from bacteria. If you have a very hairy dog, such as a Rough Collie, you should invest in a mask to prevent yourself from inhaling dust and hair from the vast amounts that come off these types of dogs. In fact, it is prudent to use one anyway when blasting or grooming out, especially if you have any type of chest problem such as asthma, as it will prevent you getting the dirt and hair into your chest and lungs. You may want to use safety goggles also.

Always look after the health of you and your dog when grooming and never take any chances of accidents happening.

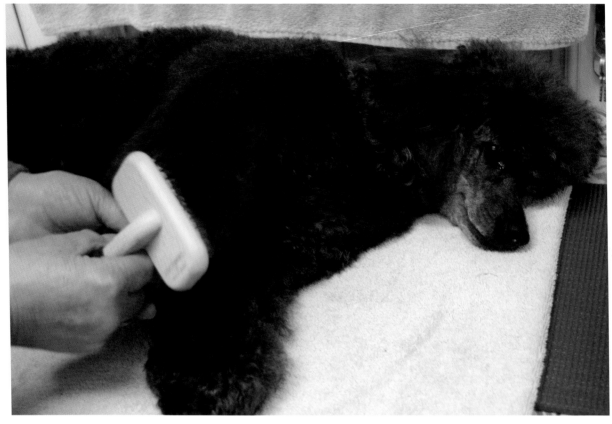

An old girl taking it easy as she gets her pampering.

Geriatric Dogs

Geriatric dogs come with their own set of problems for the person grooming them due to their inability to cooperate for any length of time if required to stand. They may, in the time required to groom them, need medication or food or water and it is important that this is adhered to otherwise the dog may suffer severe consequences. These dogs need special care and should be handled gently and with empathy. In general, I would always choose to clip off an old dog, whether or not it was my ideal style, rather than make it stand for hours to be bathed, dried and then have to be cut, which would mean that the poor animal would need to stand even longer. The exception would be if they had an easy coat. It is really not fair to ask too much of an old dog. The priority for them must be to get them done really quickly with the minimum stress imposed. An older animal should always be made

as comfortable as possible, so it might be a good idea to allow them to lie on a padded cover when they do not need to stand up for grooming.

Remember too that an older dog may have kidney problems, diabetes or other diseases and might need access to water periodically throughout the groom as well as more comfort breaks outside. It always amazes me to be told by owners that their dog is not allowed to drink too much water as it is wetting a lot when, in fact, this is the wrong thing that should be done. The dog is not wetting because it is drinking a lot – it is usually having to drink to replace the excess water that it has passed and failure to do so can damage the kidneys further. It is a good idea to let an old dog sit on the table for as long as the grooming process allows. Instead of lifting the feet and legs up they can be carefully draped over the side of the table. Under the pads can easily be trimmed in this position without stress or discomfort to the old dog. The

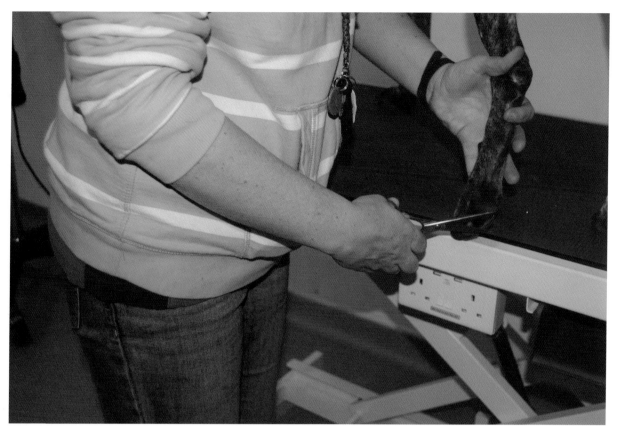

Make it easy on the joints of arthritic dogs by putting your table up so there is no need to lift the leg up high.

dog should also be given extra time to move from one position to another as they cannot coordinate or move about like they could when younger. Sometimes, especially if an old dog has thinner hair or sensitive skin, it is a good idea to use a softer type of brush as it could very easily suffer from 'brush burn', which is caused by the scraping of tender skin. Depending on the type of hair the dog has, a softer slicker, comb or even a bristle brush could be used.

Disorientation

Due to mental impairment, blindness or hearing difficulties, animals may be confused. Always speak before you touch an old dog – especially if they are asleep – as, if you touch them suddenly, you may get bitten if the animal is startled. A confused dog often emits a feeble bark too. Blind dogs should be spoken to at all times when grooming so that they can locate your position. Always take the

time to secure geriatric dogs on a table to prevent them falling off as they tend to wander around sometimes during the grooming process. This can put them at risk of falling off with disastrous consequences, as you cannot hold the dog when using your hands to groom and keep it on the table all of the time. Hearing problems are less of a problem than sight problems; however, always try to approach any geriatric dog from the front rather than from behind so that they are not startled when you handle them. I do tend to talk to deaf dogs as I believe they feel the vibrations of your voice and find that this has a soothing effect on them.

Arthritis

Arthritis is the roughening of the ends of the joints that causes pain on movement and most older animals suffer from some degree of this. Some may have or have had previous joint problems in their younger years too,

Table 1 Health Check.

BODY CONDITION	SKIN & COAT
LUMPS & WARTS	MUCOUS MEMBRANES
EYES & EARS	NOSE
TEETH	ANAL AREA
MAMMARY TISSUE	NAILS & FEET
MOVEMENT	URINATION & DEFECATION

COMMENTS

causing more pain now they are older due to arthritis. When grooming this type of animal, it is important to realize that they may cry out if their legs are handled in an awkward fashion that interferes with the positioning of the joints. Gentle handling therefore needs to be used every time. These dogs may even bite uncharacteristically if they start to feel pain. Be very careful with geriatric dogs when lifting or moving them, to avoid distress, and try to find an alternative position if it is uncomfortable. Some old dogs suffer from painful disc problems which, again, can cause pain when moving the head or lifting. Be very careful too when bathing them as they often shake their heads, causing pain in any damaged disc area, particularly if it is causing problems in the neck. It is especially important to always use a non-slip mat in the bottom of the bath for the old timers.

Health Check

A weekly health check is a good idea to do, especially with older dogs. This can identify problems that, if left, could become serious and even cause the death of the dog eventually. It is amazing what information you can pick up from your dog if you examine it regularly, not only about problems, but about what is normal for your animal, for example the size and shape of testicles in a male, the size of eyes and position of tail to name a few. Here is an example of a check that you could follow.

Skin

As mentioned earlier, as a dog ages, the skin becomes thinner, making it more prone to damage. Therefore a more gentle approach is needed when grooming. Bare patches are common on certain breeds with hormonal deficiencies too. Warts are an extreme source of annoyance as they inevitably get nicked by combing or brushing. Breeds such as Poodles often develop warts on their faces when they get older so it is obviously better to try to avoid them when using electric clippers so that they do not multiply. Very large warts should always be removed by a vet to avoid injury to them.

If any lumps grow quickly they should be investigated by a vet as soon as possible. Be very careful not to cut into any of these. Veterinary advice is needed as soon as possible to avoid spreading if it turns out to be malignant.

Often lumps are not noticed until you are grooming the dog, so it is a good idea to do that little health check as described. It is useful to keep an eye on any problems that might creep up unnoticed. Parasites are more of a problem in older animals as their immune system is often not as good as when they were younger, so it is prudent to check for these at each groom. Fungal infections and lice can be common in older dogs too.

Teeth

Tooth decay and gingivitis, as you are probably aware, can be a real problem in an older animal. Sometimes an effective cure for the disease is to have the offending tooth or teeth removed, scaled or polished as the bacteria on these teeth can affect the rest of the animal's system if left. There are times, however, that this solution may not be possible due to the health of the animal, particularly if the kidneys or liver are not functioning adequately as most anaesthetics are excreted by these organs. There are different anaesthetics that can be used depending on the status of your animal and a vet would be more than happy to discuss this with you. It is therefore very important to check the condition and functioning of these organs prior to anaesthesia. This is the reason why a vet will often suggest a blood test before doing the procedure – to assess the status of them.

If you are unsure about allowing your pet to have a dental procedure just because your animal is old, but they have a mouthful of teeth exuding pus from the gums, ask yourself if you would like to live with the pain of toothache and infection in your mouth or take a chance to be pain free, be able to eat again and enjoy a happy old age. Sometimes, if there is infection in the mouth, the vet will give a course of antibiotics prior to doing a dental procedure. The infection from teeth can travel round the body and restrict the function of the organs too. There are also various products available that can be added to water or sprinkled in daily food that help to prevent build-up of this plaque and keep the dog's teeth looking clean. This, with the addition of specialized dental chews that can be given daily, all add to the overall health of a dog's teeth and mouth care, and can stop the owner from having to smell the offensive odour from the mouth; although this is not always because of the teeth.

Some breeds have flatter feet than others but, in some, it is because of old age.

Feet

When a dog gets older, the pasterns get more floppy and the feet often become flatter. This allows the toes to stop being in contact with the ground quite so much; therefore, the natural wear and tear on the nails becomes lessened. The nails of an older dog often seem to grow much quicker and longer, which in itself sometimes causes distortion of the feet as the nails grow sideways when they get too long. It is really important to check and cut an old dog's nails regularly to prevent this happening and to avoid penetration of the pad by the nail turning inwards.

Epilepsy

Epilepsy can be a problem that is sometimes encountered when grooming your dog if it is not on medication to control the problem. It may be that the dog only suffers from this condition on infrequent occasions; however, it is always prudent to keep an eye on these dogs when you are grooming as the sensation of brushing (touch), drying (noise) and stress may be enough to spark an episode. Look for signs such as drooling or the dog staring into space, as this behaviour can be a precursor of a fit. If this occurs, stop grooming, place the dog in a quiet area and switch off any lights. Do not speak to or touch the dog either, but put down some padding, either bedding or towels, so that the dog will not injure itself if it does fit uncontrollably. Try to reduce any sensation to a minimum as this can increase the stimuli to the dog's brain and keep the episode going longer than necessary. If the fit continues longer than usual, seek veterinary advice.

Often a dog will be thirsty or hungry after having an epileptic fit. It is alright to let them have something to eat and drink; however, do not continue with the groom as the dog will usually be very tired. It would be wise on this occasion to speak to your vet prior to grooming again, although this is not an emergency unless the dog does not come out of the fit as usual or you have major concerns about its welfare.

Heart Disease

Heart disease can be quite common in older animals but sometimes even youngsters have heart murmurs or other cardiac problems. Sometimes dogs may be on medication; however, this is not always the case. If your dog has, or you suspect it has, any problems of this kind, it is very important to monitor the dog throughout the grooming process. Sometimes dogs will cough after any sort of exertion or stress. Although you may not realize it, the grooming procedure can be a source of stress even with the best of intentions and kindness from the person grooming. Anything that raises the stress level of the dog has the potential to cause a fluctuation in the function of the heart of an affected animal.

When grooming, it is a good idea to check the mucous membranes on the inside of the cheek or lips during the groom, to ensure they are staying nice and pink; if there are any signs of them being pale or blueish, stop the process immediately. This is a sign that your dog is not getting enough oxygen into its bloodstream to supply the organs, including the brain. Do not continue if this happens and give the dog a break to recover.

Incontinence

Incontinence can be distressing for a dog and owner alike if not properly dealt with. Sometimes a vet can prescribe a syrup to be given to the dog to help with the situation but the reason for the dog being incontinent needs to be investigated so that the problem can be helped. From a grooming point of view, the best option for these dogs is to shave off as much hair as possible from between the back legs, to prevent the hair becoming soaked with urine or faeces. Often the skin will become sore if the urine is left in contact with it so a water repellent product like petroleum jelly or another barrier cream should be applied regularly to stop the irritation, the area washed frequently and the product reapplied.

For urinary incontinence in male dogs, a belly band can be used along with a sanitary pad inside it to prevent the urine soiling carpets, flooring and so on. The pad needs to be changed or checked regularly. Again, it is necessary to keep the area clean to prevent nappy rash occurring. Always remove the hair that is in contact with the urine by clipping with a #7F blade (*see* more about blades in Chapter 2) closely to the skin.

21

CHAPTER 2

Tools of the Trade

Main Equipment for Grooming Dogs

As a novice groomer or pet owner it is very important to understand the range of grooming tools that are available and how they are used. I have often had owners arrive at my salon with a matted dog and, when asked what equipment they are using, they produce a soft baby brush. It is therefore no wonder that the coat was not being sufficiently groomed, as these types of brush do not penetrate longer hair effectively. The method of using tools is important too and sometimes the techniques take a little practice.

This chapter will show you the equipment required for grooming and trimming a dog. You don't need to go all out and get the top of the range tools; however, they need to be of good enough quality to do the job effectively. It is much more difficult to try to cut hair with blunt or inefficient scissors that cause no end of frustration. Not all of the tools will be required for each breed, so judicial selection is important if you do not want to waste money.

Brushes

The Slicker Brush

The basic tool for most dogs is a slicker brush. This is a brush that has small metal pins protruding from a cushion-like pad. The pins are slightly bent near the tip, allowing them to 'grip' the hair. Slicker brushes are available in many varieties according to size, pin softness or pin length. They also have the option of small plastic tips on the end of each metal pin to prevent injury occurring. It is important to select the correct type of slicker brush for the coat you are dealing with to prevent injury to the dog or damage to the coat. Slicker brushes can be used on most coat types, although care should be taken with smooth coats and show dogs for reasons that will be outlined later in this chapter.

The slicker should be held lightly and used quickly, always brushing from the ends of the hair towards the root. The brush should not come into contact with the skin as it will cause a graze; however, it is important to brush the hair at the roots thoroughly. Care should also be taken not to brush the same area for too long as this will result in 'brush burn' damage. As said previously, this is where the top layers of the skin are removed due to brushing too hard or too long in one place or by using the wrong hardness of brush. The use of hot dryers while brushing can also speed up the rate at which brush burn can occur. Slicker brushes accelerate the drying time of the coat by allowing the separation of each hair and letting the air circulate more efficiently through its thickness. Great care has to be taken on sensitive areas like the groin, anus or nose. Special care should also be taken around any bony parts like the knuckles, elbows and hocks as these have very little hair covering.

OPPOSITE: Grand old lady Katie deciding on what tools would be best for her double coat. The one you cannot do without is the blaster.

The most important tool in the groomer's box. The one you cannot live without.

Wool Coats

Slicker brushes are particularly useful for wool coats as they are excellent for the process of 'fluff drying' breeds such as the Bichon Frisé, Poodle or Bedlington Terrier, or any wool-cross breeds such as the Cockapoo or Labradoodle. This is because the brush can be used to gently pull the coat straight as it is being dried. Fluff drying is a process that stretches the hair out to enable scissor work to be completed to as even a finish as possible. A straight coat, with each hair completely separated from the next, is an essential foundation to finishing and scissoring these breeds.

The brush will also help to remove matted hair caught up near the skin. Wool breeds do not cast their coat in the same manner as other coat types but they do still cast old coat, contrary to what some breeders may tell you. Individual hairs still reach the end of their lifespan and are shed from the skin, but the wool coat around it gathers together at the root, forming tangles among the living hair. This type of coat must therefore be regularly brushed out to prevent matting. A wool type of coat actually needs more attention to grooming than other types, unless they are going to be clipped short.

Double Coats

Double-coated breeds, for example Rough Collies, Newfoundlands or Alaskan Malamutes, have a shorter, very dense undercoat and a longer topcoat that sits up off the body. Slicker brushes are useful for removing dead coat in these types. They can also be used to break up any felting of the undercoat near the skin although it is recommended that a blaster will do a better job in the first instance. Slicker brushes can also be used in conjunction with a de-matting tool to remove mats from the feathering.

Silky Coats

Silky coated breeds would be Setter and Spaniel types. They have some undercoat and a longer, fine topcoat that lies flat against the body. Slicker brushes can be used on the feathering to brush the leg and belly hair and can help to remove mats. They also be used on the back and head in a gentle manner to remove dead coat and knots. Be careful though if you are using them on a show dog as you do not want to lose any long coat. Dogs with a silky coat do not have an abundance of undercoat and therefore can suffer from brush burn much more easily. A softer type of slicker should be used on these coats. In the case of any thinly coated dogs it may be prudent to use one with plastic ends on the tips to make sure they are not getting scratched by the pins.

Wire Coats

Wire-coated breeds, such as West Highland White Terriers, Scottish Terriers and Italian Spinones, usually have a good undercoat and a longer, wiry topcoat. As with silky coated breeds, brushes are used to separate hair, brush out any matting and remove dead coat. Wire-haired breeds generally have more undercoat than silky coats therefore a slightly firmer brush may be required.

Smooth Coats

Smooth coats can have a little undercoat and a short, tight topcoat that lies flat to the body. Examples of these dogs are Boxers, Dalmatians, Labradors and Weimaraners. Great care needs to be taken if using a slicker brush on these breeds as they can easily suffer from brush burn, especially on bony areas like the hocks and elbows. A hound glove or rubber brush may be more appropriate for these breeds. A hound glove fits over the hand and can have plastic or rubber pimples or bristles on the palm area. The dog is stroked with the glove or rubber brush to remove dead coat and undercoat.

Pin Brush

When it comes to long show coats, slicker brushes can break and damage them so should be avoided where

An essential tool to remove all that loose hair on smooth coats. You can also use it on your carpets to catch the hair you missed when grooming.

as dogs that are in show coats are not usually matted or tangled. Pin brushes are not effective on neglected coats. A pin brush removes the minimal amount of hair when grooming.

No coat should be brushed when dry. A good-quality grooming spray should therefore be used prior to brushing any coated dog as the hair is more elastic when wet, so no breakage should occur and it should minimize hair damage.

Bristle Brushes

Bristle brushes are super for putting shine on a dog, especially the pure bristle type, but they are not for everyday grooming purposes. Once a dog such as a Spaniel has been thoroughly groomed, de-matted and is clean, a bristle brush can be used on the muscular parts of the body to produce a great shine. They are not suitable for wool coats, however.

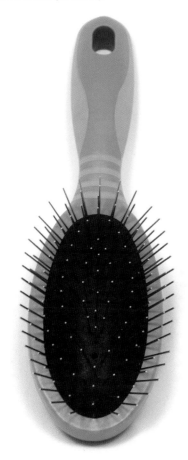

A gentle brush for the dogs with precious locks. Only for use where there are no knots present.

possible; a pin brush is therefore usually used on this type of specialized coat. Long-coated Lhasa Apsos, for example, may be brushed with a pin brush as long as there are no knots in the coat. This is usually possible

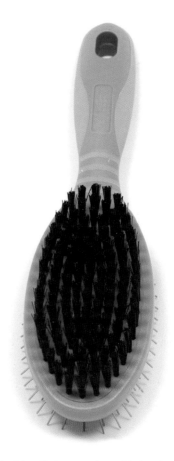

Combined with a little coat gloss, this brush will help your dog outshine the rest if they have a silky coat.

Rakes

Conical Rakes

Shedding tools can be used on double-coated breeds such as Samoyeds, German Shepherds or Collies. They should be raked through the coat in the direction of coat growth as this will break up and gather dead and felted undercoat. It should not damage the topcoat. These are not tools to be used on show coats that are having regular maintenance. They are excellent for use on the coat of a Curly Coated Retriever.

Blade Rakes

These can be used for removing dead undercoat from smooth coated breeds such as the Dalmatian or Labrador. They can also be used on the fronts of the legs to assist with carding (scraping out the dead undercoat to clear the colour) a silky coated Gundog but not on the feathering. The tool should be used lightly in the direction of hair growth. However, again, great care needs to be taken over bony areas, and any areas with sparse hair should be avoided, for example down the tendon, above the hock. The tool is not suitable on wool coats.

De-Matters

De-matters come in many forms and can be useful for mats on any coat type. The type of tool preferred will depend on the preference of the groomer but whichever

Use this with care to avoid scratching the skin. However, you will be impressed with how much loose hair it will remove from short and medium coats.

No grooming box is complete without this essential de-matter. If used correctly, you will whisk out those mats in no time.

This unique configuration helps remove that stubborn loose undercoat by raking it out without cutting.

The previous de-matter's baby brother. Smaller but just as effective for cutting up and splitting the mats.

one is chosen, it must be used carefully and in the correct manner. Some de-matters have several curved blades with a sharp inside edge. They should be used with short, sharp strokes working from the outer edge of the mat in layers towards the skin so that you are not trying to bring a mat into a mat. Be very careful that the blades do not come into contact with the skin as injuries could occur. Neck and throat areas are best avoided with this tool unless you are very experienced. There are also mat splitters available that have several long, straight teeth with serrated edges coming out of the handle. These are used by placing the teeth between the skin and the mat, then using a sawing motion away from the dog's body to break the mat again into several pieces; this makes it easier for the mat to be brushed out with a slicker brush or comb.

Combs

Combs come in a variety of sizes and teeth spacings as well as different tooth lengths and grips, and can be used on all coat types.

Long-Toothed Combs
These are useful for longer coats such as on Newfoundlands or Standard Poodles. The length of the teeth on these combs makes it much easier to comb to the skin and they are available with or without ergonomic grips

General Purpose Combs
This type of comb has teeth of two different widths on the one comb. This enables the groomer to loosen off tangles initially with the wider side and finish off with the narrower one. The choice of comb should be suitable for the coat being groomed. You would not use a coarse comb with wide teeth to groom the fine coat of a Yorkshire Terrier or use a fine one for a Newfoundland.

Banded Combs
Combs are also available with wooden or plastic grips in place of one half of the length of the comb. This type of comb can be altered by tightly intertwining a thick elastic band round the teeth, giving you what is known as a banded comb. This is extremely useful for getting the loose hair out of silky coated dogs when hand stripping the coat.

From the flea comb on the left to the finishing comb on the right, there is a task for them all.

Make it easy on your hands with this specially designed handle for your comb.

The easiest and kindest way to remove dead and loose coat on Gundogs with silky coats.

Flea Combs

These are ultra-fine combs that can be used to locate fleas in a dog's coat. They will catch the flea in the teeth but make sure you quickly dispose of it when you find one before grooming another part of the dog. These combs can also be used for removing fine undercoat if necessary.

De-Shedders

De-shedders can be used to remove dead hair and undercoat from wire-coated breeds or some silky coated Gundogs that are to be hand stripped but not being shown. They should not be used on any feathering as they will very quickly shred it. They are also useful on neutered dogs that have grown a very thick coat as they remove the excess, allowing the coat to lie flatter against the body. A de-shedder should be used in the direction of coat growth only, as if it is used against the growth, it will result in the coat being cut. De-shedders are available as single- or double-sided and in fine, medium and coarse tooth spacings. Although people do use them on double coats, they often tend to remove or cut the hair, leaving bald patches. They should definitely not be used on wool coats.

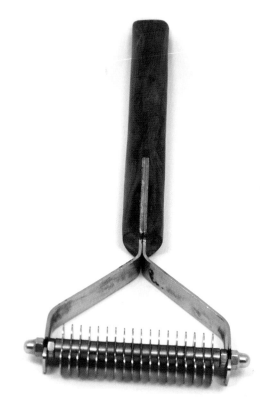

The ultimate tool for neutered silky coats and for de-bulking wiry coats prior to stripping.

Stripping Tools

Stripping Knives

There are many different types of stripping knives favoured by individual preference. We will cover the most basic type here as it is most relevant to the pet owner. Stripping knives are used mainly on wire-coated breeds and come in fine or coarse versions and also right- or left-handed types. When they are used to hand strip coats, the coarse blade is usually used for the body and the fine blade for the ears. The blade is held in the hand at an angle of approximately 45 degrees to the skin and a few hairs at that time are trapped between the thumb and knife. The hair is then pulled out in the direction of the hair growth. Be very careful to only pull the top layer of hair and not the undercoat. Using the knife at a 90-degree angle can cause the hair to be cut rather than be pulled out cleanly and therefore this should be avoided at all costs.

Knives should not be used to strip silky coated breeds but may be used to card these coats instead. Ideally you would use a proper carding knife to do this, but they can

Quite a range of stripping tools. One for every scenario. Some breeds are stripped at different times over the body to get the optimum look.

be used on wire and silky coated dogs to remove dead undercoat. The stripping or carding knife should be gently used, flat on its back, in the direction of the growth. Stripping knives can also be used on smooth coats to clear the colour but should never be used on wool, silky or double-coated breeds.

Stripping Stones

These generally come as a large block and can easily be broken into manageable pieces by using a comb to push down onto it and snap it into hand-sized pieces to suit the individual. They are used to remove untidy or unwanted hair on wire-coated or silky coated breeds. Stones are used by gripping high up on the stone and curling the fingers to ensure they do not move about as you work,

causing blisters on your palms. The top hairs are trapped a few at a time between the groomer's thumb and stone and are drawn out in the direction of hair growth, just like the stripping knife. The hair should be grasped at the tip and not next to the body as, if you do so, you will pull out the undercoat, causing a bald patch. Gripping the hair too low on the shaft will not only result in the undesirable pulling out of the undercoat but also bruise or pinch the dog's skin. Loose skin should be stretched out before the hair is stripped from it. Stripping stones cannot cut the hair in the same way as stripping knives so may be preferable to use for the beginner. Stripping can also be done with rubber finger stalls or, indeed, finger and thumb if the coat is of good enough quality.

Scissors

Foot Scissors

These small scissors are used for trimming under and between pads and around the foot and eye areas. They consist of two straight blades with smooth, sharp edges. Some of this type have a rounded tip so that there is less chance of injuring the dog with sharp points.

General Purpose Scissors

This type are of variable lengths and widths to suit breed and groomers' preference. They can be used for scissoring larger areas. These again are composed of

This useful stone can be used on most coats, except wool, to get rid of cast hair.

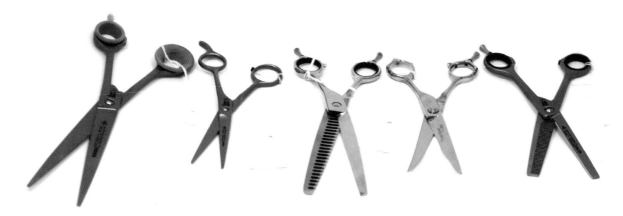

Straights, foot scissors, chunkers, curves and thinners. They are all there.

two straight blades with smooth edges. They sometimes can have serrated edges to the blades that give a better grip.

Finishing Scissors

These are a longer type of scissor and are used for fine scissoring of Poodles, Bichons and so on. They are very sensitive to knocks and are not suitable for scissoring thick or heavily coated areas or double coats, but are only used to put a fine finish on wool coats.

Curved Scissors

Curved scissors are very useful when creating a round shape, for example Bichon heads or rounded feet on Lhasa Apsos, and are composed of two curved blades with smooth, sharp edges. They are available in various lengths depending on what kind of dog or area you want to use them on.

Single-Sided Thinning Scissors

These are used to blend areas of clipped coat into longer hair to leave a natural finish or to de-bulk thick, heavy areas with excess hair. They are constructed of two straight blades, one of which is smooth but the other has a comb blade edge.

Double-Sided Thinning Scissors

This type of thinning scissor can be used to create texture on West Highland White Terrier heads, for example, or to de-bulk thick coats. They are constructed of two straight blades with a comb edge on both.

Chunkers

These scissors are used for creating texture on heads or scissoring chunky coated breeds. These are composed of two straight blades with a very coarse comb opposite a smooth blade. These types of scissors are not, usually, used to blend long into short, unclipped areas on finer coats, but to give a rougher, more rugged look on coarser coated breeds.

It is really important when choosing scissors that they fit your hand comfortably. It is therefore better to buy where you can try them if possible. If this is not an option, get in touch with a reputable supplier for advice. Cheap scissors from the internet or budget shops will not be suitable for grooming your dog as they often are not good enough quality to cut the hair of a dog efficiently. Poorly made scissors can cause all sorts of wrist and hand problems too.

Scissor Exercises

The following are some scissor exercises that you can practise to enable you to use your scissors correctly and effectively. You will not find them easy to begin with – no one does. Keep going, however, and you will wonder how you cut any other way.

Scissors should always be held on your ring finger, next to your little finger, and on your thumb. The thumb should be bent with only the tip on the ring and never be pushed any further through the hole. Make sure your scissors are up the right way. Most scissors have a little-finger rest on one side so this will help you know which way up they are.

Starting with your scissors upright against a wall, stretch your blades as wide apart as possible without dipping the tips inwards. Repeat the opening and closing process until your muscle at the base of your thumb gets stronger. It will feel quite strange to begin with until you get used to it.

When you have practised the opening and closing exercises, rotate your scissors in a 180-degree curve on both sides while still opening them and closing them as wide as you can. Make sure the whole of the blades on your scissors remain the same distance from the wall at all times. This will form the basis for your control of the scissors when cutting or scissoring your dog. It is advisable that you learn to do this so that you can cut a straight line and have proper control of the scissors around delicate areas.

Clippers

Clippers can be corded or uncorded, which are battery operated. The clipper choice is a personal preference but many people look for a clipper that is lightweight and slim enough to hold comfortably in your hand for a few hours, and is capable of dealing with a thick coat. Clippers can be single speed, two speed or variable speed. Variable speed gives the most flexibility, as the speed of the cutter on the blade moving back and forwards can be adjusted depending on requirements and the thickness of the hair. This is useful, especially if the coat is matted. There are many different makes and shapes of clippers on the market and most will come with a universal-type blade fitting. That means that if you buy another set of

clippers your blades should be interchangeable. All clipping is done with the growth of hair unless otherwise specified. Take note that using clippers against the coat will result in a much shorter bald patch.

Trimmers

Trimmers are lightweight clippers that can usually be powered by a battery or attached by a connection to the mains. The purpose of trimmers is for clipping the hair short in certain parts of the groom, including the ears, as they are much quieter than the usual type of clippers. This can be useful if you are clipping near the face as the dog may not resent them as much because they are cooler and do not have as much vibration. These are indispensable for clipping a Poodle's feet, face and tail and are certainly a must if you are going to clip this type of dog. The blade that is used with these type of clippers is interchangeable for length. It uses only one universal blade that can be adjusted by moving the lever at the back from a #9 setting to a #10, #15, #30 and finally a #40, which is the shortest. These are usually used when the area to be clipped is quite sensitive or the length is to be short.

Blades

These are numbered to allow identification of cutting length and can be either full toothed or skip toothed.

Full-Toothed Blades

These have every tooth the same height as the rest and will have the number of the blade followed by F or F C. This type of blade gives an even, smooth cut and is the most commonly used type of blade for most popular styles.

A hard-working general purpose clipper. You select your blade to attach to it. Do not forget to have them serviced regularly.

The ideal trimmer for dainty, close shaves; one blade for everything, from #40, #30, #15, #10 to a #9 setting.

A #7F would be the blade used for clipping off a coat that was matted or where a short back coat was required on a breed like a Cocker or Springer Spaniel. If a slightly longer Terrier groom was wanted, a #5F or #4F could be used.

Skip-Toothed Blades

Skip-toothed blades have every second tooth half the height of the one next to it and do not have a letter after the number. They give a more ragged cut and can sometimes be used on clipped Terrier coats. All blades #9 or shorter do not have a letter but are full toothed. In dog grooming, the length of the cut of the clipper blades is dependent on which blade is used. The higher number on the blade, the shorter it will cut the coat; therefore a #5F blade will leave more hair on the coat than a #7F and a #7F will leave more hair on than a #40.

Blades can have either a ceramic cutter or a metal cutter. There are advantages and disadvantages to each. Metal cutters are more robust and they can be sharpened when the edge goes dull many times before the end of their life. Ceramic cutters are very fragile and will not survive being dropped. They do not, however, overheat like the metal cutters and stay sharp for up to ten times as long. When they do go blunt, though, they sometimes cannot be successfully sharpened and the cutter has to be replaced.

The blade should be checked regularly while running to ensure it does not become too hot or reaches an uncomfortable temperature for the dog to bear against its skin. An overheated blade can cause a burn and damage or irritate the skin. Blunt blades also snag or pull the hair rather than cutting it, which can also cause irritation of the skin. Blades must be regularly oiled while grooming by applying a light application, at frequent intervals, between the cutter and the blade, to reduce the friction between them, thereby preventing a build-up of heat on the blade. It is imperative that the blades are not left lying out, as condensation in the atmosphere will cause them to rust. They should be cleaned, oiled and stored in a blade box or in a clean, dry towel to protect them. Any blades with damaged teeth should be discarded or new parts purchased.

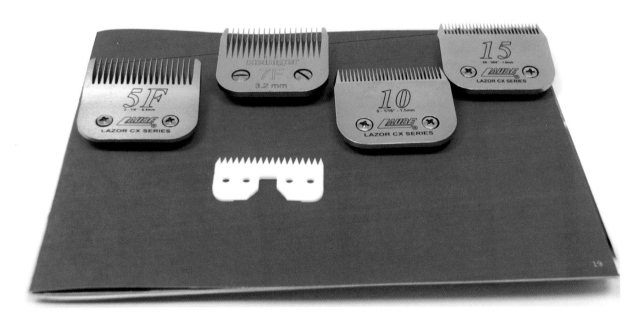

The main blades and ceramic cutter for general grooming. Remember to keep a spare of the size you use most often so that you can send it away for sharpening without being without a blade.

Table 2 Blade Chart.

Common blade sizes	Common applications
40 Leaves about 0.25mm of hair	• Poodle face, feet and base of tail; can be too short on sensitive skins • Clipping mats from under pads
30 Leaves about 0.5mm of hair	• Poodle face, feet and base of tail; can be too short on sensitive skin • Under-comb attachments for puppy/teddy trims
15 Leaves about 1.2mm of hair	• Poodle face, feet and base of tail • Under-comb attachments for puppy/teddy trims
10 Leaves about 1.5mm of hair	• Under-comb attachments for puppy/teddy trims • Ears
9 Leaves about 2mm of hair	• Miniature Schnauzer body • Cocker Spaniel when #7F is untidy
8.5 Leaves about 2.8mm of hair	• Cocker Spaniel body when #7F is untidy
7F Leaves about 3.2mm of hair	• Clipping off all coat • Clipping out under matted areas • Clipping groin area or armpits • Cocker/Springer Spaniel body • Some Terrier bodies
5F Leaves about 6.3mm of hair	• West Highland White Terrier body • Some Terriers where #7F is too short for individual • Short body styles where there is no matting
4F Leaves about 9.5mm of hair	• Shortish body styles where there is no matting, for example Lhasa Apsos
Comb attachments Always used over #10, #15 or #30 blade	Puppy/teddy styles

Comb Attachments

These can be used to achieve what is known as a 'puppy cut' or 'teddy bear cut' without the skills required to scissor well. They can save a vast amount of time over the more traditional scissoring techniques and, in some breeds, can also be used to make a rough shape prior to scissoring. Comb attachments are particularly suited to drop-coated breeds such as the Lhasa Apso, Tibetan Terrier and Bearded Collie. Dogs requiring use of a comb attachment need to be bathed, dried and completely free of knots and mats before any clipping is started. Failure to remove all the knots will result in the comb snagging on the hair, causing some of the hair to be cut much shorter than the surrounding hair and the comb getting stuck in the hair. Care needs to be taken as well to ensure that the comb and blade do not build up an accumulation of cut hair as this can ruin the cut too.

Comb attachments are fitted over a #10, #15 or #30 blade. They cannot be used on any longer blade without causing damage to the comb. Each attachment will have the length of cut coat stamped on it. The clipper blade is fitted to the clipper body and then the attachment is carefully fitted, neatly and securely, to the blade by slipping the lugs on the bottom of the attachment over the bottom of the blade, and then gently pushing the comb attachment up until the teeth fit over the blade.

When the clippers are switched on, there should be no excessive noise or rattling. On occasion, comb attachments can be used against the growth of hair but, in general, they are used in the direction of the coat. Cutting

It is so easy to shorten coats with these bad boys. A length to suit all sizes of dog.

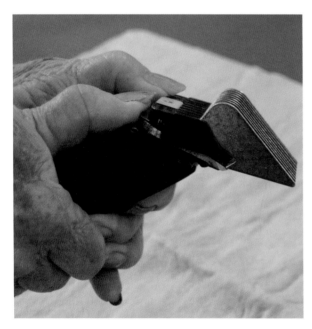

Slip the spring-loaded clips over the blade for an easy groom.

across will remove chunks of hair and show patches when finished. The coat grows along the spine towards the base of the tail and the sides grow downwards usually, so this is the direction to follow. Never use comb attachments in the groin or armpits.

A puppy cut or teddy bear trim is a style that is basically the same length all over with, perhaps, slightly longer leg hair depending on the taste and requirements of the owner. The one rule for this or any trim is that, to achieve balance, the body hair should never be longer than the leg hair as the dog begins to look like a footstool rather than a well-groomed dog. This is an area that distinguishes between a professional groom and that of someone who has just attempted to take the hair off randomly or for convenience; balance is very important to the overall aesthetics of the finished groom.

As mentioned previously, the comb attachments are used on top of a #10, #15 or #30 blade only. It is also important to use them on a conventional clipper and not a trimmer. Sometimes trimmers are sold with comb attachments too but great care needs to be taken as they have a tendency to spring off while clipping, resulting in a very, very short patch of hair. The bottom of the attachment is spring loaded and fits neatly under the bottom edge of the blade. Comb attachments are usually sold in sets of varying lengths. When choosing which comb attachment to use, lay out your whole set on a table in order of length. The general rule is that for larger breeds, the longer combs from the middle length upwards will be suitable. Smaller dogs can usually have combs from the middle size down to give a successful finish.

Sometimes, if you are going to use a really short comb attachment, a longer blade – such as #7, #5 or #4 – on its own may give a better finish. You can, of course, play about with the length until you get the look you want. Always try out the length on the rump with a longer comb than you think you would like, as you can always go down a length without compromising the trim and it is easy to blend in if not to your liking.

Care of Equipment

It is really important to look after your tools to extend their life and to prevent them from rusting or damaging the dog's coat. The other reason for looking after your tools is to prevent infection to the dog or you, by cross contamination. Most households will not have access to sterilizing equipment; however, in most cases, this is not a problem as items like brushes, combs and rakes can simply be cleaned efficiently by removing any hair from them and then by washing them in hot soapy water. After you have done that, use an appropriate tool sanitizer that can be bought from grooming suppliers. This is sprayed onto the tools and can be wiped, then left to dry. This will get rid of any germs that are likely to cause a problem in dogs by contact. It also gives you a chance to check for any breakages or worn areas that would necessitate the need to replace the item, as broken tools, missing teeth or broken pins can scratch the dog's skin and cause infection and also not enable the tool to work efficiently.

When cleaning blades and clippers, remove any excess hair or debris that has accumulated in them before cleaning. A good way to do this is by using your blaster to get rid of all of the hair in the crevices. Blades can be cleaned by using a suitable product available from grooming equipment suppliers and following the instructions on the label. This degreases and cleans the blade. Wipe the blade and apply a small amount of oil to lubricate the cutter. Remember: if you are using metal equipment that has elements that move back and forwards over each other, it is very important to apply oil regularly to prevent the parts welding together. When one metal moves against another it causes friction, which, in turn, causes heat. Sprays are available for disinfecting too, but be careful not to inhale any of the fumes if using on a hot blade.

Scissors of all types can be wiped with surgical spirit after cleaning off any hair; take care as they can be extremely sharp. Clean the blades and shanks thoroughly and, after applying a small amount of oil to the fulcrum, leave to dry.

Comb attachments are a little more tricky to clean but can be scrubbed with a soft brush and hot soapy water to remove the grease that builds up on the teeth. Once this has been done, you can spray them with tool sanitizer and leave them to dry. It is very important to keep your tools out of reach of any moisture. They should therefore be stored in a damp-proof container and out of sunlight. You can buy blade boxes with lids that are excellent for keeping them safe.

Scissors are best kept in their original case or a case or wrap that can hold a selection of them. This will prevent your scissors becoming chipped or damaged by getting knocked; they should be treated carefully, since they can be damaged easily and a slight knock or being dropped can cause them to cut inefficiently. The tips of scissors are often the part that gets blunt first due to them being the thinnest. Scissors are carefully balanced during manufacture and can be upset by the slightest bump, so place them on the table carefully. It is very important that you do not use your dog-grooming scissors to cut anything other than dog hair. Explain calmly to your family that your scissors are strictly out of bounds for cutting paper, cable ties or twine.

Cost of Equipment

As a groomer of your own pet, it is not necessary to buy the top-of-the range tools for everyday use. However, it is important to invest in a decent quality. It will be a much more difficult job to try to cut your dog's hair with scissors that you need to use over and over for them to cut, than with sharp blades that cut the full length of the shaft. It is advisable to speak to some of the more prominent grooming suppliers about your needs rather than buying something at random from the internet. I often have students arrive with a selection of tools they have bought without knowing what their use was. They have never used most of them and have had to re-buy, as they have been such poor quality.

Just a final point: do not be tempted to buy scissors because they look bejewelled or are a fancy colour. This is not the reason you are buying them. They need to be functional and reliable. Remember that most good-quality scissors do not need fancy packaging to attract you to them.

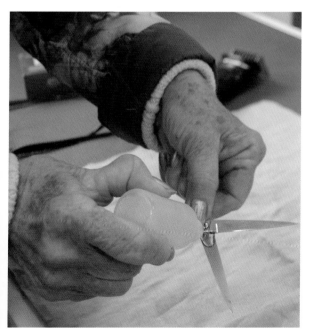

Get into the habit of oiling your blades and scissors even when you are grooming.

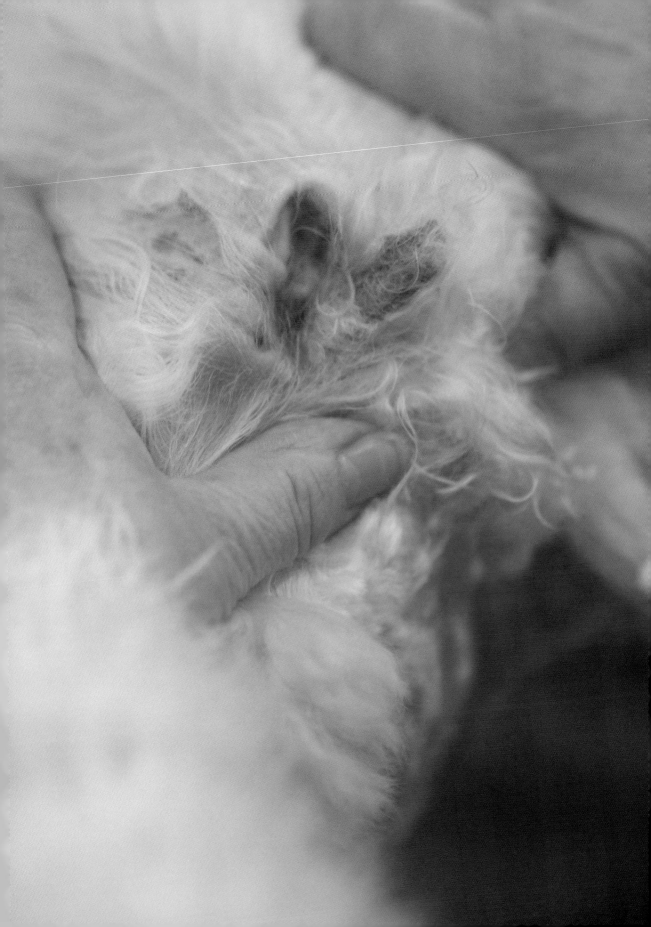

CHAPTER 3

The Delicate Bits

The Structure and Purpose of the Skin

The skin is one of the most important organs of the body, as its role is to prevent damage to the internal tissues through contamination from infectious substances like bacteria, viruses or general dirt that can be picked up daily. It also prevents water, nutrients and bodily fluids from being lost to the exterior of the body, where they may be evaporated off. Many particles come into contact with the skin daily, through normal movement or close contact with substances that are all around us, but these are prevented from infiltrating the outer membrane of the well-designed waterproof covering of the body. This is effective on most of the body except in a few delicate areas like the inside of the eyelids or lips, where the outer layer of skin is much thinner and is more easily penetrated by unwanted substances. This is the reason they look more pink and moist, and – as the nerve endings are nearer to the surface too – are more sensitive to stimuli. The structure of skin allows it to be very elastic and this property enables it to stretch and bend without splitting.

The skin is divided into three basic parts – the epidermis (the outer layer), the dermis (the middle layer) and the basal layer (where regeneration takes place). The new cells that form in the basal layer are small, but as they start to mature, get larger and then become the dermis, which is relatively young and healthy. The epidermis or superficial layer contains the most mature cells that have become, or are starting to become, old and dry. These cells start to scuff off and are shed as skin scales.

In the dermis, which is underneath the outer layer, there are important structures that serve to maintain the function of the skin and coat, and are responsible for aiding the operation of other major organs too. The dermis contains muscle clusters that enable movement of the body and include 'erectile muscles' that are found on various parts of the dog's body, but mainly along the spine. These muscles are usually used when a dog wants to show another dog that it is larger or more dominant than it, and these erect hairs are usually referred to as 'hackles'. In another situation, hairs can be made more erect if the dog is trying to prevent heat from escaping from the body. Warm, heated air is trapped in the puffed-up coat of the animal, like the effect of a duvet. If it was not for the outer layer of skin, these muscles might get damaged, with dire consequences to the dog.

The lymphatic system is also found in the dermis, and is where potentially damaging substances are removed from the body, through the blood supply and into a network of channels called the 'lymphatic system'. These are filled with a substance called 'lymph'. There are also a few glands in the dermis that are attached to the hair follicles. The sebaceous gland is one of these and this produces sebum (a waxy substance that covers the hair shaft), especially when the dog is stroked or brushed. As you can imagine, this makes the hair shiny, sleek and glossy.

OPPOSITE: There is plenty of hair in this canal. However, the dog is very reluctant to let anyone take it out. This is probably a vet job under sedation.

A sleek and shiny coat on a well-nourished dog. Plenty of stimulation of the sebaceous glands helps to coat the hair with a shine-enhancing substance called sebum.

Other glands in the dermis are sweat glands. These are not, in general, useful for heat removal but, in fact, disinfect the skin. Salt water is a good disinfectant and this is a natural use of the product for cleanliness. The only real place that sweat is used for dissipation of heat in the dog is on the pads of the feet, along with panting, which uses evaporation of water from the tongue to cool down.

Throughout the skin there are cells called 'melanocytes' that produce melanin, which helps to protect the skin from the effects of too much sunlight. In most white dogs, as with fair-skinned humans, sunburn can be an issue and, therefore, darker skin offers more protection than pink as it contains more melanin. In some breed standards, a white version of the breed should have silver or darker skin; however, some dogs may have a mixture of pink and black or dark patches on their body. Eye rims and noses are also less vulnerable if they are black, or at least as dark as possible to offer good protection yet again. Vitamin D can be important and meat is the usual source in canines, although it is made to a degree from the action of sunlight on the oils on the skin or hair. Lack of vitamin D can cause the health of the coat to suffer as well as more serious health problems in the dog.

Understanding Coats

Knowledge of how various coats are formed and their constituents is a valuable lesson if you want to understand the grooming process. The reason behind the need for different tools and techniques to be used for grooming different dogs and coats then becomes apparent. There are usually two different types of coat that occur in dogs and both appear in various degrees in each breed. The first is the undercoat, which is a softer, thicker type of hair that is formed next to the skin and is where mats can easily form. It is the coat that keeps dogs warmer in cold conditions; it is obvious, therefore, that breeds that are likely to have originally been kept in colder climates or outside, usually are the breeds that are going to have most undercoat. Unfortunately, when these breeds are kept inside in warm homes, they try to get rid of the excess heat by casting their coat constantly, often much to the distress of their owners.

Coats are such an interesting topic as breeds have at least five distinctive types. These are wool, double, smooth, wire and silky. In addition to these there are also hairless dogs that grow very little hair at all and some only in specific places, for example the Chinese Crested.

Dog hair is composed of a protein called keratin, which is the same one responsible for tusks, nails and so on. This construction is arranged as a shaft of hair with barbs shooting outwards from the main stem. These barbs, when placed side by side, catch onto each other unless the hair is not well conditioned. These spikes catch onto more hairs and eventually a mat develops. With the use of conditioner, the spikes of keratin become flattened against the hair shaft, making it less likely knots will form, as the hairs cannot get the opportunity to catch onto each other. The same thing happens when the coat is brushed and the sebum coats the hair shaft, again flattening the rough outer covering of the hair. That is why the coat develops a gloss and tangles are minimized when brushing a coat.

Hair Growth

There are various stages of coat growth in dogs. These are anogen, catagen, telogen and exogen. The first of these, anogen, is when the hair is actively growing. The next stage is catagen, when the hair starts to mature before proceeding to the next stage. Telogen is next, when the hair growth is static and is what is referred to as being 'in full coat'. The last phase of growth is exogen, when coat that is finished growing is shed or expelled so that new, fresh coat can take over from the duller, aged hair. Sometimes this coat just falls on the floor easily but in breeds such as wool coats, it needs to be removed by grooming as it tends to just accumulate at the roots and will mat if left. The other problem that happens if this unnecessary coat is not removed is that the skin does not get any exposure to the air and this often results in skin problems. The coat starts to look dull and dusty, eventually hanging in clumps like a camel shedding its coat. The method of removing this coat depends on the breed and coat type.

Dogs tend to have a cycle of growth that is seasonal. However, if the weather is warmer than normal, the animal may get rid of excess coat so that they can remain cooler. Conversely, if the weather is unseasonably cold, the dog may regrow a thicker coat to compensate for this. The other reason a dog will shed its coat unnaturally is if it is living indoors in a centrally heated house. This is especially a problem with breeds such as German Shepherds and Malamutes, who will often pant constantly and shed masses of coat in an attempt to get much

cooler, and sometimes want to lie on a cool, tiled floor to help the process. They like nothing better than to be allowed to go outside whenever possible to be in a natural environment.

I hope this gives you some insight into how and why a dog's coat behaves the way it does, and the reason once again why you need to groom your dog on a regular basis.

Nails

Nails are made from a protein called keratin. This is the same substance that makes up hair and horn. Like all other body substances, the quality of the keratin is dependent on good nutrition. Well-nourished nails

These nail clippers make nail cutting easy unless the dog has long quicks.

39

prevent damage during the growing process. Nails form from the nail base and grow continuously, sometimes seeming to grow faster in an older dog. In the middle of most of the nail lies a blood vessel commonly referred to as 'the quick'. The quick comes to a point and is covered over by a layer of keratin. There is a little hook at the underside of the nail that is a good indicator of where the quick ends, so you can gauge where to position your nail clippers. It is very important that nail clippers are held in the correct position and are angled so that the quick is not cut by mistake.

There are two types of nail clippers commonly available for cutting a dog's nails: the guillotine type and the side-cutting type. There is sometimes a slider to help minimize the chance of clipping the quick as it only allows a small amount of nail through the gap at a time; however, there will always be a time where, for various reasons, a quick will be bled and subsequently will need to have the bleeding stopped. This can usually be easily be dealt with by applying styptic powder. This is a substance that encourages a wound to close together quickly and stop any bleeding. This powder is sold under various names, such as Trimmex, Clip Stop and Stop Quick. A little of this powder should be applied to the bleeding nail and then left alone, as any interference only causes the clot to move and for bleeding to start again.

If styptic powder is not successful in stopping the bleeding, soak cotton wool in really cold water, hold it onto the nail and apply pressure. Cold water will cause the blood vessels to contract and therefore the bleeding should stop. These accidental bleeds usually stop quite quickly but, in the event of this not happening, it may be necessary to take the dog to the vet, who may apply a pressure bandage for a few days.

There is a nail that is situated at the inside of the leg and this is called the 'dew claw'. Dew claws are what are left of another toe from earlier times. Gradually, this claw has become smaller on dogs, resulting in some puppies not having them at all; however, most puppies will have them. It used to be customary to remove these claws before the puppy was three days old and, in docked breeds, this was usually done at the same time as the tails were cut. Docked breeds often included working Gundog and Terrier breeds, although Poodles were docked too. This may have been due to the fact that they were often used as water retrievers. Often these dogs got their tails damaged when working through undergrowth and the end of the tail had to be surgically

This is how the nails curl round and corkscrew if left to their own devices.

removed, as they did not heal well and often got damaged again. Nowadays, dew claws are much smaller in most cases, but sometimes they appear again in a larger form and can also show up on the hind legs too. These hind dew claws can also be double and in some breed standards they are desirable.

From a grooming point of view, dew claws tend to be a nuisance when brushing and combing the legs as they can get caught between the teeth of the comb. Therefore, if your dog has them in place, please be careful when grooming this area. Vets will not usually remove these now unless they get damaged, as many dogs go through life with them without experiencing a problem. It is the hairier breeds that usually give cause for concern when grooming with a comb or clippers, so always make sure you check for these prior to grooming. Sometimes you may notice that the dew claw has grown into the leg. This can be a real issue in some dogs that only get the nails on their feet cut (and not the dew claw on the leg). Dew claws have the potential to either grow round in a corkscrew fashion or actually grow into the leg. It is important that these nails are cut out of the twist, but if any of the nail has started to go through the leg, the dog needs to get it removed by a vet as it will require an antibiotic to prevent infection and often there will be quite a bit of swelling, possibly with pus around the area.

Check when you are grooming for any brittle, broken or split nails that are very easily torn. Like human nails, they can be helped by good nutrition and a little care. A good treatment for these types of nails, in fact any nails, is to use hoof-care ointment that is used in the treatment of horses. This can help to strengthen the structure and prevent the nail breaking. It is advisable to do this as a regular task at each weekly groom. Nail-bed infections can be a real problem and will need treatment by a vet, as often there is an infection from the area from which the nail grows. You might see brittle or broken

areas right next to the skin, with the area around usually being reddened or inflamed. It is worth checking these areas at each groom, as getting the problem solved early is often the key to a successful cure.

While you are examining the nails, it is also prudent to check between the toes for any tiny red or orange dots. These can cause intense itching and the dog may well be biting at its feet. These are usually known as harvest mites for which your vet can prescribe a wash that will alleviate the problem. While you are looking between the toes you may find evidence of blister-like cysts too. These are interdigital cysts and can be very painful ('inter' meaning between and 'digital' referring to fingers or toes). There is often a lot of matting between toes and under pads that can obscure the view of these cysts so dig deep with your fingers if the dog has very hairy feet. The removal of these mats will be covered in Chapter 6. Sometimes, under the pads can be cracked and sore; if this is the case, you can apply a little foot balm that can be purchased from a vet or pet store.

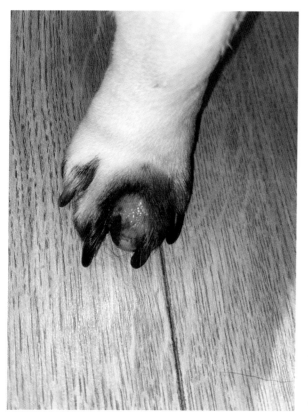

This shows clearly how painful interdigital cysts can be. This one is on a French Bulldog.

Ears

Ear Shapes

There are various shapes of ears that occur in dogs and, unfortunately, some can become a source of many problems. Spaniels have teardrop-shaped ears that hang down closely to the sides of the face. These allow very little air into or near the ear canal and therefore are very prone to causing infections. Erect ears that stand up from the head, like those of a German Shepherd, are not so prone to problems, as they are wide open and have good airflow into them. Semi-erect ears stand upwards at the base but fold over at the tip, for example those on a Shetland Sheepdog. Rose ears are seen in breeds like Pugs and Greyhounds. These ears are convoluted and resemble a tightly curled rose when you look into them. The French Bulldog has a type of ear referred to as bat ear. This is wide at the base and narrower at the rounded tip. Another type of ear is what is known as a butterfly ear, found on the Papillon. If you look at the dog from the front, the head and ears resemble a butterfly.

Ear Cleaning

To understand problems of the ear, it is necessary to understand what the ear actually looks like and how it works. The ear is quite a complicated organ. Hairs inside the ear constantly waft debris and wax upwards towards the ear flap. This process works really well assuming the ear canals are reasonably wide. When the canal is narrowed, it prevents air from entering the ear to keep it fresh and the old debris from being able to work its way upwards and out of the canal with the help of the internal hairs. When this happens repeatedly and starts to cause problems, a vet may perform surgery known as an aural resection. This operation is only performed as a last resort as, usually, the application of drops alone will clear up the problem. This operation involves making an opening from the canal to the underside of the ear, where gravity lets the detritus drain out, keeping it healthy. In most cases, however, ears are treated using easier methods.

When cleaning the ear, always use a cleaning solution specially made for animals; do not use water or any other products because they may injure the ear as they may not be a suitable pH for the dog's skin. Sometimes if a dog is very prone to waxy ears, the vet may prescribe a liquid to flush out the ear.

The method for cleaning ears is as follows: squeeze the recommended amount of wash into the ear and use your fingers to squelch the underside of the ear, thereby massaging the fluid inside the whole ear and canal. Once this is done, the excess wax and dirt can be removed with cotton wool. The procedure can be repeated until no more dirt comes out. Sometimes it may be a while later when you will see more debris inside the ear as it is being wafted to the outside by the small cilia or hairs. Never put cotton buds inside the ears as there is a good chance you could damage or even burst the ear drums.

When doing a normal, routine clean of the ears, remember to use one piece of cotton wool in one ear before discarding it into a waste container; then use a second piece for the other ear. This avoids the risk of transferring any infection from one ear to the other. Put the ear-cleaning liquid onto the piece of cotton wool and clean inside the ear, wiping around the folds, as well as cleaning the whole ear flap. Take a good look at the ear and check for any redness or thickening of the flap and internal surfaces. The dog may shake its head if it has an ear irritation so, if the ear smells, this is not normal. It may have a brown discharge that is possibly crumbly or, in a severe infection, pus running out of the ear. This will be extremely painful for the dog and veterinary treatment is needed immediately. If you examine the ear you will find that there is a little flap at the back of it that opens up to expose the inside area. Check this routinely

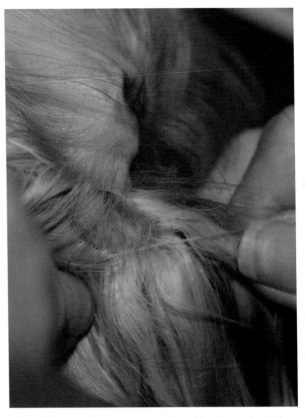

A few hairs at a time are removed, making it comfortable for this little dog.

as this is often where you will find lice. These are small, sesame-seed-shaped parasites.

There are some breeds that grow a large amount of hair in their ear canal and this can interfere with the function of the ear. It may be necessary to remove this hair as long as there is no discomfort to the dog. Special ear powder can be bought that enables you to get a better grip of the hair and keeps the ear fresh and clean. A little powder should be puffed onto the hair; then, plucking a few hairs at a time, remove the hair from inside the canal. Never attempt to cut this hair. If the dog is not comfortable with the procedure, you should stop. In this instance it may necessitate a trip to the vet to get the hair removed while under anaesthetic.

Teeth

Teeth are very important in a dog as, being a carnivore/ omnivore, they need to have the ability to rip up, chew and grind their food into pieces that are small enough to swallow. Each type of tooth has a different function. The incisors are the front teeth that pull or rip the chunks of meat off the bone or shred a larger piece of meat. The premolars and molars chew and grind the meat down in the same way grain is ground between two large pieces of stone when making flour. To work efficiently, the surfaces of the teeth need to be in the correct place, otherwise the latching on of the incisors and surface-to-surface grinding of the molars will not happen satisfactorily.

In a puppy, there are twenty-eight deciduous teeth. These are teeth that fall out at a few months old and are replaced by bigger, stronger teeth. There should be forty-two adult teeth in a perfectly formed mouth; however, some breeds have gradually lost their premolars, or if they do have them they are very small. Over the years, these premolars have become unnecessary for the dog to successfully eat their food or carry their prey. This being said, forty-two teeth are always deemed desirable. A perfect mouth for most breeds is where the top teeth are very slightly in front of the bottom teeth but with no gap, and this allows the inner surface of the top teeth to rub against the outside of the bottom teeth. This also

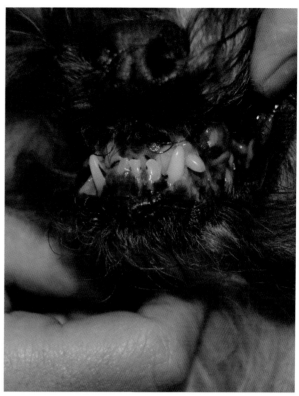

This little dog will have more of a problem eating with this undershot mouth.

enables the dog to be able to get a good grip of the food or prey and hold it in place. In the past, some dogs had what was referred to as a level bite, where the surfaces rubbed against each other. This was quite effective too but caused excess wear and tear, eventually causing the teeth to wear down easily and shortening the amount of tooth above the gum line.

Other issues can occur with a dog's mouth and can pose a problem when both eating and keeping the teeth clean. One problem is what is referred to as an overshot jaw or 'parrot mouth', where the top jaw is too far in front of the under jaw; the two surfaces of the teeth are therefore very far apart. This can cause a problem with being able to grip with the front of the mouth, and also the bottom teeth may dig into the roof of the mouth. The opposite issue occurs when the bottom jaw sticks out in front of the top jaw. This is called an undershot jaw.

Teeth should be placed in an even manner in the gum with no teeth out of alignment. Often this is not the case and the teeth are all over the place. In a puppy, there may

A beautiful set of teeth in this little toy Poodle. A perfect scissor bite, too.

This mouth shows deciduous teeth being pushed out to make way for the adult teeth.

be problems with the teeth being in the wrong place or the deciduous teeth not coming out in time for the new teeth to come in correctly. In these cases, the deciduous teeth should be removed by the vet as soon as they advise it and ball therapy can be used.

Cleaning the Teeth

It is imperative to make sure all surfaces of the teeth can be reached when cleaning them to allow debris to be removed. Examination of the mouth should be done first to check for loose teeth or infected gums; if these are present, the dog needs to go to the vet for a dental examination and treatment. Redness and swelling around the gums, with or without any signs of pus being there, is a sign of gum disease. This will probably cause the dog to be in some degree of pain and possibly not want to eat. Imagine how you would feel with continuous toothache. It is not fair on the dog when owners do not get their

dog's teeth attended to regularly, especially when they get older.

Owners often worry that their dog is too old to have an anaesthetic when they have really bad teeth but surely, if the vet thinks it is reasonable to do so, you should take the chance to give the dog a pain-free life for the time it has left. Even if the vet will not do a dental – and this is very rarely, as anaesthetics are so advanced now that they pose very little problem to older dogs – they will often prescribe antibiotics to get rid of the infection.

Method

You can use a soft children's toothbrush or one specifically for dogs with specially formulated canine toothpaste. This is easy to obtain from larger pet stores or vets. Vets also sell packs that include all the necessary equipment for tooth cleaning. Get your puppy used to this from an early age by doing a small amount of brushing regularly

Early training to accept having their teeth brushed can go a long way in keeping the teeth good for as long as possible.

and often. Gradually extend the time so that, when the puppy becomes comfortable with the process, the whole mouth can be done in a session. You can buy a brush that you can slip your finger inside, which may be preferable to a puppy. Just make sure the puppy does not mistake this procedure as a game, and keep the initial sessions short.

Some toothpaste is flavoured with chicken, beef and so on. This makes it more enjoyable although some dogs like the original flavours. Each dog is different so make sure the process is as easy as possible by giving them their favourite flavour. When you are brushing, make sure you brush the insides and awkward places too, where debris can collect. There is also a dental wash that is easy to use and can be put into drinking water

to prevent plaque building up, meaning there is less chance of tartar forming on the teeth.

Ultrasonic tooth-cleaning systems for dogs are available and they can be very effective. This service may also be offered by some grooming salons for an extra charge. This method uses ultrasound to remove tartar, plaque and staining. This works really well, especially if used regularly. Make sure the system is one specially designed for dogs if you would like to use this method. The only criteria when using this is that you must be sure the teeth are not loose, or the gums infected, so that there is no risk of doing further damage to the mouth. Cases of loose teeth or infected gums must go to a vet to be treated.

CHAPTER 4

When Problems are Uncovered

There are times, when grooming your dog, you will come across unusual areas in the coat or on the skin. It is quite important that you recognize what is normal or abnormal in dogs. The following are a few of these circumstances, to help you identify when you need to be concerned or not.

Warts

Warts are pretty common in dogs, especially as they get older, and are caused by what is known as the papilloma virus. This virus is easily spread from one area to another on a dog's body. The canine papilloma virus, like others, does not usually infect other species, so poses no risk to humans. The warts are often small and can be caught by a comb when grooming, causing them to bleed and contaminate the surrounding skin. In most cases, these warts are benign – that is, not cancerous – and do not normally pose a real health problem in the dog apart from being unsightly and inconvenient. If you knock the top off a wart it is wise to stop the bleeding as soon as possible by using styptic powder or liquid skin to form a cover over it and prevent it spreading to the area around it. Some warts can become large and are a nuisance when grooming as well as being unsightly. It is usually best if these are removed on the recommendation of a vet rather than being continually damaged.

First you have one and now you have lots. If a wart is damaged, the virus spreads to the area nearby and more warts appear.

OPPOSITE: Such a beautiful dog but who knows what is lurking under that thick coat.

Tumours

Often owners will come across a lump on their dog when grooming; however, not all lumps are malignant, and the majority pose no problem to the dog long term. Many breeds, especially Gundogs for some reason, tend to get fatty lumps as they get older. These fatty lumps can grow really big and, whilst not malignant, can cause physical impairments to the dog by either rubbing, causing irritation or preventing the dog from moving normally. These are obviously best removed on these occasions.

Other types of lumps that the owner may discover are mammary tumours. It is good practice to always examine the mammary area of your bitches routinely. Feel along the undercarriage, going quite deeply into the tissue. Some lumps in this area will be glandular, especially in an un-neutered bitch after a season, but some may have the potential to be or become malignant. Often it is in the area near the hind legs that these tumours first appear, but

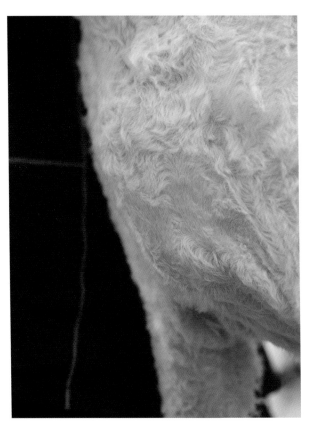

Lipomas can appear anywhere but are commonly on the breastbone.

not always, and they could be found anywhere along the line of mammary tissue to right underneath the front legs.

These lumps need to be seen by a vet and not self-diagnosed. If suspicious, usual treatment will include removal and examination of the lump in a laboratory. If malignant, the bitch will usually be spayed to prevent spreading by the release of hormones that are produced when they come into season. On some occasions, the best option is a mammary strip where all the mammary tissue will be removed on either one or both sides. These surgeries help to prevent the tumour cells moving into the lymph nodes and therefore spreading to other areas of the body. Do not mess with this type of lump if it is found. Seek the advice of your vet as soon as possible and the chances are you will still have your bitch for many years.

If you have a male dog, make a habit of checking the testicles too. If you do this regularly, you will be familiar with the normal size and shape for your dog. If there is any change in these areas or if you discover your dog has none or only one testicle, a trip to the vet is the best policy. If a dog has a retained testicle, it is important that it is removed to prevent the missing one becoming malignant. The reason the testicles hang outside the body is that it is a cooler environment and this is necessary for the testicles to stay healthy. If the testicle is kept inside the body, it will be too warm and cause cell changes to the detriment of the dog.

Always check the anal area too. Look out for a fishy smell or any lumps around the anus. Anal gland problems are very common and should be suspected if there is a distinct smell around the anus or if the dog is dragging its bottom on the floor when it tries to relieve itself of the pressure from the fluid inside. The dog might also keep biting at its anal area. In the past, groomers were allowed to express anal glands but now the best solution is to go to your vet where they can examine them to determine if they have an abscess or only need emptying.

Mites

Ears are often a source of problems in dogs, especially if the ears are of the downward hanging variety, where it is difficult for air to get into the orifice to keep them healthy, as mentioned in Chapter 3. Many breeds grow excess hair inside their ear canals that can cause problems with the normal function of the ear. For many years it was normal practice to remove this hair completely with fingers and ear

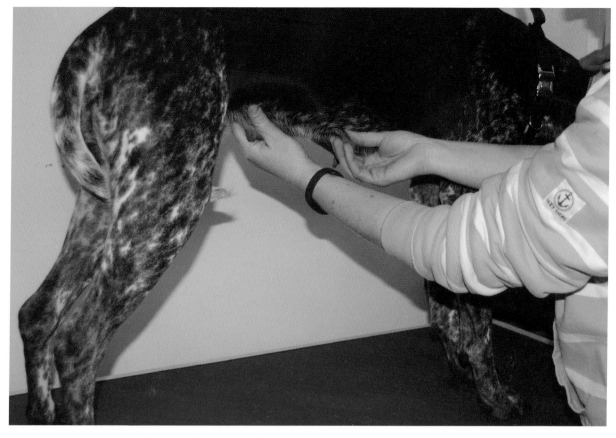

Breast screening makes you better safe than sorry. Regular check-ups are beneficial for dogs too.

powder, but now, again, the advice is only to remove any that comes away easily and not to probe down into the ear canal.

Ears should not have a nasty smell or discharge. Signs of otodectis externa include redness, itchiness, brownish discharge and possibly thickening of the ear flaps and a foul smell. This is caused by a mite called otodectes that crawls about the inside of the ear, causing intense itching to the dog resulting in the scratching process further damaging the ear. This can cause bacterial infection on top of the mite problem. Ears should be checked routinely when grooming and there are many good products available to keep them fresh and clean. It is important to use these products properly.

Conjunctivitis

It is a prudent exercise to always add examination of your dog's eyes to your grooming regime as well. Many problems can be picked up early and improve the chances of cure by just taking a few minutes to include this in your routine. You may even prevent a dog from going blind in some cases. Any discharge from the eye can be caused by numerous problems. Conjunctivitis is quite a common cause of irritated eyes and the discharge will look as if there is pus in it. Again, the vet can prescribe an antibiotic that can clear it up quickly. Often there can be redness too, especially if the dog is rubbing its eyes or pawing at them.

Parasites

The very thought of your pet having lodgers brings the fear of death to many people but, by understanding how these parasites live, you can help avoid a minor problem becoming severe. The general understanding of a parasite is that it is an organism that lives off another

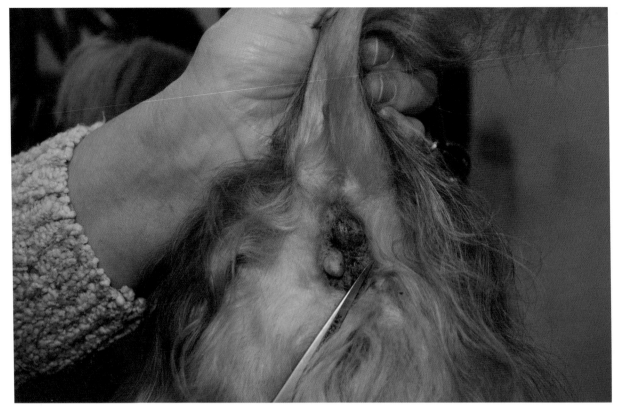

Anal problems here as you can see. This can be a common place for growths.

organism to the detriment of the host, sometimes with fatal consequences. There are some contradictions to this in that there are some organisms that coexist with their host where both receive benefits from the union.

The Flea

The very mention of a flea makes people itch with just the thought of them. In an animal-owning household there are probably fleas there all the time, but only when they become a nuisance do people know they are there. The first indication is probably an itchy bite or two. Nowadays, many dogs are treated for parasites regularly but sometimes the flea population seems to exist and cause trouble regardless. In reality, as the flea does not live on the dog but only goes on to feed, the problem can be the surroundings it is living in. Our modern lifestyle is a perfect, cosy, luxury pad for a flea: central heating, fitted carpets, sumptuous furnishings, cosy multi-tog

duvets and furry rugs. What better place to cuddle down, lay your eggs and rear your children. This is exactly what the flea does. It is especially at home in crevices of skirting boards, between cushions on sofas and in corners of dog beds.

Some dogs are able to withstand a large number of flea bites with little or no problem but others are very sensitive to even one flea. If you think about it, if you find a flea on your dog, there are hundreds more in the surrounding area so the treatment there is a must to eradicate the problem. Regular vacuuming is an effective way of controlling the population, as well as cutting down on comfortable furnishings (for example have wooden floors rather than carpets). However, before we all need to go back into a cave to be free of them, we can do lots to help the situation. Regular treatment can go a long way to breaking the lifecycle and treatments are readily available from your vet who will know which is the most suitable for your pet. Bear in mind though that fleas are the intermediate host of the tapeworm.

Lice

Lice are little bugs that look like sesame seeds. They are usually found behind and at the ends of the ears but can be found anywhere on the dog if the problem is severe. These parasites do not leave the dog to breed, unlike fleas, so they are much easier to treat. Not all dogs get lice and, in fact, two dogs from the same house may not both be affected. Often it is puppies, older animals or sick animals who are susceptible and, in these cases, the immune system is possibly not functioning as well as it could be. Probably the most effective treatments will be obtained from your vet who, again, will confirm the presence of lice. Lots of dogs have scaly skin at the bottoms of their ears that can be mistaken for lice, especially Spaniels.

Ticks

These bean-shaped parasites are very common, especially in areas of moorland where deer or sheep graze. Often they will latch onto anything that passes, and that includes humans. They can cause lots of problems including anaemia and Lyme disease. Lyme disease is a very debilitating illness that can last for years and sometimes for life. Ticks can be easily seen and are very similar to a little cream-coloured bean. Sometimes, when they are small, they can be mistaken for a wart. After they latch onto the host, dog or human, they begin to fill up with blood, therefore enlarging in size. When they have had

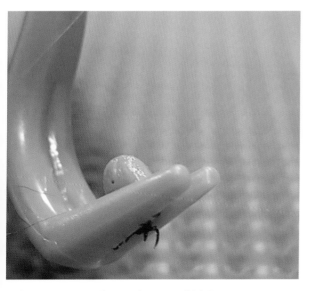

Ticks are a source of Lyme disease, which is very debilitating, so wash your hands and dispose of ticks properly after handling them.

their fill, they drop off to digest the meal and remain on the ground until they need to feed again.

It is very important that ticks are removed properly as, if the head becomes detached from the body, they may cause an abscess. It is possible to purchase tick removers easily at most pet stores. These catch the tick behind the head; then, when turned anticlockwise, they cause the tick to let go of its grip. Never pull the tick away from the skin. Always check that the whole animal has been removed prior to disposing of it. You could dab a little antiseptic powder or lotion on the area the tick was attached to if you wish.

Skin Problems

When you are grooming your dog, you may find that there are areas of the coat or skin that look abnormal. You may find that the coat looks unusually scurfy. This can be due to a dog casting at certain times of the year or after having a litter, but it may also be that the dog is in too hot an environment. There are excellent coat and skin supplements that can be purchased on the internet or from pet stores that can help enormously if the dog is lacking in any vitamins or minerals. If your dog has a scurfy coat, look carefully at the scales – just make sure you don't see any moving. If they are, the problem could be due to a parasite commonly referred to as cheyletiella or 'walking dandruff'. If this is the case, you need to get treatment from your vet if they confirm that this is the problem. Poor health can also cause a dog's coat to be scurfy, so if this is the problem it should clear up when your dog is better.

If you find bald patches in the coat, there can be quite a few reasons for this. If the patch is round with a red rim, and has broken hairs around the edge, it is important that you wash your hands and wear gloves as the problem may be a fungal infection called ringworm. This can be transferred easily to other animals, including humans, so it is imperative that all areas are disinfected well and all grooming tools cleaned and decontaminated too.

There are other skin problems that can be passed to humans too and one of these is sarcoptic mange, otherwise known as scabies. This is a little mite that burrows under the skin, causing intense itching. If in doubt about any skin complaints with dogs, always err on the side of caution by wearing an apron or overall and latex or rubber gloves when handling the dog. Finally, wash your hands thoroughly.

Often people find that their dog has a greasy or oily area along its back that is difficult to get dry. This is usually caused by overactive sebaceous glands that produce the product called sebum that lubricates the hairs. Again, the vet can prescribe a treatment for this or there are also very good degreasing shampoos available from suppliers. One problem that can be a real nuisance is when your dog rolls in fox dirt when out on a walk. It is notoriously difficult to remove both the smell and oiliness. A well-established natural cure is to apply tomato sauce onto the area and rub it in, then shampoo as normal. It works a treat every time.

If a dog starts to lick its feet for whatever reason, this can become a really annoying habit that is difficult to stop. Sometimes dogs will do it because of an allergy and they will continue to bite and chew their feet throughout their life. White dogs are very prone to allergies. This can be due to many things including grass, pollen, food allergies or intolerances or contact with certain floor coverings. The list is infinite and it is often very difficult to get to the bottom of the problem. There are good products available from your vet that can help with seasonal and long-term allergic conditions but often it is an uphill battle to get it totally under control.

You may find that your dog has got tar on its coat or feet. If this happens, rub some butter onto the areas and wash

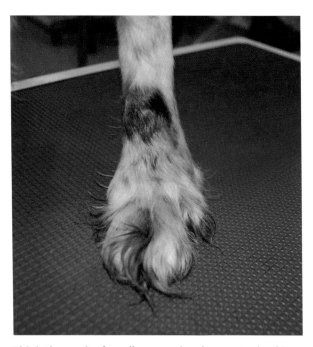

This is the result of an allergy causing damage to the skin due to the dog constantly licking the leg.

thoroughly with warm water and detergent. This might need to be repeated to get all of it off but is very effective.

There are a few health problems that can show up on the skin that may be caused by hormonal problems. In a condition called Cushing's disease, the skin can get quite thin over the back and sides of the dog and the dog often has a distended belly. Sometimes crusty plaques appear on the skin too that can flake off when grooming, so care is needed here. The dog may drink a lot and urinate more too. This condition can be easily kept under control by medication that is reasonably inexpensive but needs to be monitored well to begin with to get the optimum dose.

There is yet another condition that can be indicated early on by observation when grooming: an underactive thyroid. Among the symptoms of an underactive thyroid is the presence of a tail that has very little hair on it and is described accurately as a 'rat's tail'. There will be other signs, probably including lethargy, but this tail is most distinctive of the problem.

Note that all dogs have a gland in the middle of their tail that is sometimes very conspicuous in breeds like Border Terriers, West Highland White Terriers and sometimes Labradors. This is nothing to worry about and is normal. With careful grooming you can leave a little hair over this area to cover it if you find it offensive.

Finally, if when you are grooming your dog you come across bruising or blood spots, it is important you take it to your vet to be seen. It may be an important indication that there may be a blood problem going on so, obviously, the sooner the dog is seen by the vet the better.

Odours

Sometimes when people are grooming their dog they complain of them being extra smelly. There can be a few reasons for this. The first one is their teeth may need attending to so have a quick look in their mouth. Doing a little health check regularly is not a bad idea as it can let you pick up potential problems in advance of them becoming a major issue. Rotten teeth are certainly a major source of a smelly breath in dogs although it can also be present if they have stomach trouble, which can cause foul smelling gas to come up regularly, a bit like indigestion.

Next in line for sources of smells are the ears. Again, this can be avoided by regular attention and cleaning with a good product, or treatment if caused by infection. Check in your dog's lip folds too, as a lot of bacteria can collect there (especially in Spaniel-type dogs), which can start an infection. Not only can this be very annoying to the dog, but it can also cause a putrid smell. Always wash this area thoroughly to remove food and old saliva.

Sometimes Gundogs, when wet, do have a particularly pungent odour that seems to be caused by the oil that protects their coat and makes it waterproof. Not a lot can be done about this problem really though as it is not practical or advisable to wash them every time they go out in wet weather. A deodorizing shampoo can be used if it is of major problem.

A big problem in some dogs is smelly feet. They can get almost the equivalent of Athlete's foot in humans. The only solution is to wash them regularly in a medicated shampoo and rinse and dry thoroughly, making sure between the toes is dried too. There are also some powders that can be obtained from your vet or pet store.

As we reach the rear end of the dog, probably the worst smell that people and owners complain about is from the anal glands – the most pungent of smells imaginable and unmistakable. They have a very fishy smell that lingers forever. It may be a sign that your dog may have anal gland problems. A problem apart from the smell is that other dogs may take a more than normal interest in them as they pass. This can be a very painful condition for the dog and they may be biting around the problem area as well. Again the vet will check what is going on and may show you how to empty them yourself if it is needed on a regular basis. Diet can help a lot of dogs with this issue if more roughage is included in their diet to bulk up the stool so that it squeezes the glands as it passes through the rectum.

Other Problems

A thing to be very aware of on the feet or legs is any sign of a grass seed becoming embedded. The area may be swollen and red and you may be able to see the end of the seed protruding from the wound. It is important that you do not try to pull the seed out, as it is like an arrow and has barbs pointing in one direction only. Another trip to the vet is required for this one. If there is any suspicion at all that there could be a grass seed in a dog, do not assume it isn't as it can travel through the body with fatal consequences. Inside the ears and the feet are areas that can be prone to this problem.

Sometimes dogs develop cysts over their bodies too that spontaneously burst and release the filling over the dog. The vet will squeeze them to remove the fluid and allow them to lie flat against the body again. This can be a messy business. These can be of the sebaceous variety, which are filled with a cheesy-type substance. It is a job for your vet to ensure it is emptied properly. Any cysts or lumps that you find should always be checked out by a vet to rule out any possibility of malignancy.

You may have noticed that sometimes a dog will develop a soft swelling on their hocks or on their elbows. These tend to be found on large dogs and are usually caused by lying on a hard surface, sometimes concrete slabs outside. What happens in these circumstances is that the body needs to protect any bony areas from any damage or pressure, so secretes a fluid to make a cushion of sorts that surrounds the bone and prevents the hard surface pressing on it. This is usually known as a bursa. Nothing needs to be done with these swellings, as if the fluid is removed the body will just secrete more. They can be unsightly but in most cases do not cause any problem.

If you are grooming your dog and it seems unsteady, stop and observe it to make sure there is no possibility of the dog collapsing, especially if the dog is old. Immediately check the colour of the mucous membranes inside the mouth to ensure they are pink. If the membranes are pale or bluish in colour, stop grooming immediately and remove the dog from the table until it has recovered or been checked by a vet. Dogs with known heart problems need to be monitored throughout the groom as they can have heart murmurs or other conditions of the heart that have an effect on the amount of oxygen being circulated in the blood.

Some other breeds, particularly Bearded Collies, have been known to be susceptible to having low blood pressure, which dips when they are bathed and they start to sway. Quite a few large dogs that we have had as clients have been prone to doing this in the bath. They seem to be fine when being groomed so try to bath as quickly as possible and monitor the dog while doing so.

As you can see, there are many things to be aware of when grooming your own dog. If problems are picked up early enough it may help your dog to have successful treatment and live a long life. It is amazing the number of dogs that come in to be groomed who have health problems that the owners have not picked up on. Abnormal discharges from anywhere, but especially from the vulva in a bitch, need to be checked out as soon as possible as it could be a case of life or death. Often this problem, called

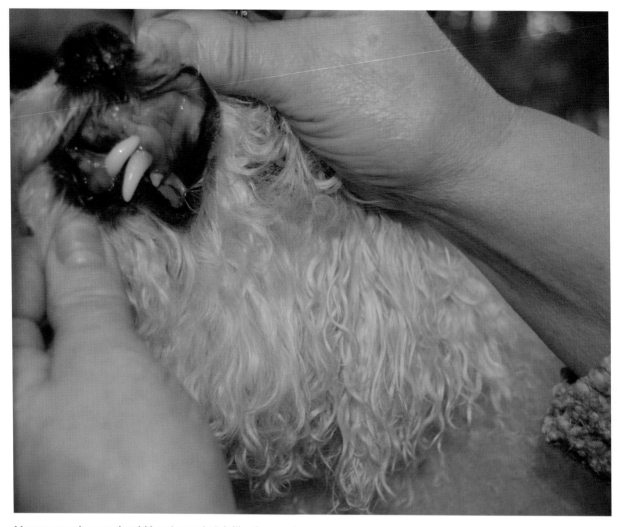

Mucous membranes should be nice and pink like they are here.

pyometra, occurs in an un-neutered bitch at about the time she would have produced pups, roughly nine weeks after she has been in season. Of course, it can happen at any part of the cycle but this is when it is most common. If a bitch constantly has false pregnancies there is an increased chance she will develop pyometra.

Lack of grooming of hairy dogs like Old English Sheepdogs and so on can be a source of hidden surprises when the coat eventually needs to be groomed. A chewed caramel, a safety pin, a needle, a child's toy and a sprig of holly are a few of the things found in the coat when dogs were brought in to be groomed. Also common are a varied selection of slugs that stick to the coat like glue.

The importance of keeping on top of your dog's routine has been obvious here. While we find some of these finds amusing, there are other objects like bits of glass, grass seeds or bits of stick that can be very dangerous as they may travel into the skin or cut the dog if not found soon enough.

Finally, have a good look at your dog when it comes off the table to check that it is standing uniformly on all legs. Feel the legs to make sure that there are no swellings or abnormal shape or position to them. Some dogs never like their legs or feet touched, but if the dog is more reactive than normal it may be because it is finding that area painful; although you cannot see anything, never ignore this. It is the same if you find your dog is being less cooperative throughout the grooming process. Give the dog the benefit of the doubt that they may not be feeling their best or may have an illness developing; you may just need to give them a couple of days to see if they are any better then. This is particularly important if your dog has had sickness and diarrhoea as they may be feeling squeamish or have an upset tummy. Usually, if there is nothing wrong with the dog after a few days, try to groom them again and hopefully they will be back to normal.

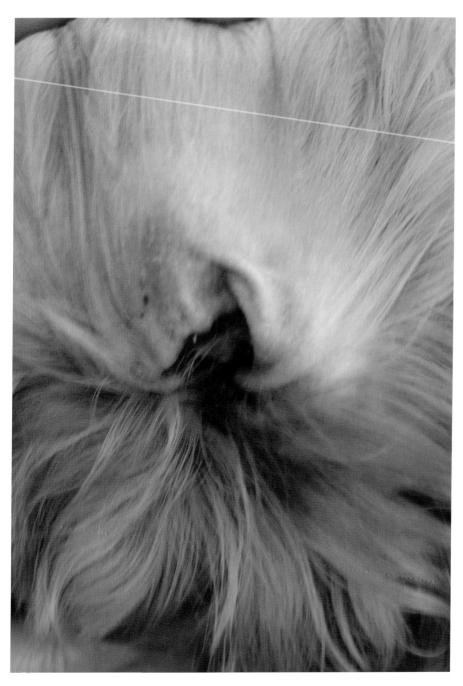

Redness and wax in this one. Some attention needed before the problem escalates.

CHAPTER 5

Bathing and Drying

Preparation for Bathing

It is important when you are bathing your dog that there are some basic safety measures in place that will prevent your dog and yourself from becoming injured, possibly frightening the dog, which may result in a phobia about being bathed again. If you are using a bath or shower, always ensure you use a rubber mat in the bottom of it to prevent the dog from slipping, which could result in a back or neck injury. Once a dog has had a bad experience, it can take quite a while for them to get over it. If it is practical, try to have some sort of restraint attached to the wall with a neck strap clipped onto it, so that your dog is not tempted to try to jump out of the bath. A large suction pad with a ring is a good choice and is both cheap and effective.

Always check the temperature of the water prior to wetting the dog and adjust it so that it is comfortable on the inside of your wrist. Bathing should be a soothing experience for the dog, the same as it is for us. I am never more amazed as when an owner tells me they wash their dog with a cold hose at the back of their house and their dog does not like to be bathed. Unless you live where the temperature is very hot all year round, you can understand why the dog does not like to be bathed.

There are a few things to be done prior to bathing the dog. First, make up your shampoo to the recommended dilution shown on the bottle. Get all your cosy towels ready for drying off and collect your equipment for brushing, drying and so on at the grooming table, so that

This is a great investment to avoid accidents in the bath, and inexpensive too.

OPPOSITE: Bath-time frolics can be fun for some but others run and hide.

you do not need to leave the dog when you have taken it out of the bath. Make sure you feel that your dog is able to be bathed as well as being clipped or groomed on the same day; if your dog is ill, infirm, old or aggressive, it may be kinder to clip one day and bath the next. This will be more pleasant for both of you and you can have more quality time with your pet.

When you are starting to groom out your dog's coat, have a quick check of the condition of the coat and indeed of the dog. This is an ideal time to do a quick health check to ascertain any changes in your dog since the last groom or bath. Check for lumps and bumps, discharges, parasites or other skin problems. This is important as it may affect which shampoo you will be using. If you suspect the dog has a skin condition that is a bit suspicious, for example itchy, bald patches with a red rim or dandruff that seems to be moving, it might be better to postpone your groom and bath until you have spoken to a vet and they have seen the dog to establish if the condition is infectious to humans or other dogs. This may also be a factor in your choice of shampoo.

To perform the bathing and drying process satisfactorily, a dog must firstly be properly prepared with all mats and tangles removed. The exception to this is when a dog needs to be totally shaved off or if the dog is being 'rough clipped' prior to bathing to remove unwanted hair or coat for the desired style. If the dog is being rough clipped for styling, only the required hair for the trim needs to remain, so the remaining hair will need to be groomed out, but not the short hair. If the dog is being shaved off completely, it makes sense to do it prior to bathing. Tangled hair is composed of the individual strands being tightly wound round each other and therefore does not allow the penetration of water or shampoo to the hair or skin to clean the coat properly. This is why knots need to be brushed out prior to washing, otherwise the dog might not be clean no matter how many times you shampoo it. Grooming also allows some of the mud and dirt to be removed before the hair becomes wet, enabling more effective results to be obtained and to get the dog sparkly clean with the appropriate shampoo.

At the beginning of any process you must make sure that the tools you are going to use are clean and fit for use. The animal should be placed on a non-slip, secure surface when any grooming is going to be done. The last thing you want is for the dog to get a fright and possibly not feel secure again or, worse still, fall off the grooming table. As mentioned in Chapter 2, to be sure the dog does not jump off the table and get injured, it is worthwhile investing in a control system of some sort so that you are free to use your hands to hold the dog for grooming purposes rather than security. An H-frame is the best option as it allows control of the front and back end of the dog. Positioning of the straps is extremely important so that it allows control and safety of the animal without pulling the dog and damaging the neck or abdomen. The belly strap should never be used to keep the dog up but only to prevent it side-stepping off the table. Likewise, the neck strap should be fitted comfortably without being too tight or pulling the dog upwards.

When placing the dog on the table, the neck strap should be fitted first, followed by the back strap. When releasing the dog, remember to take off the back strap first as, when the neck strap is released, the dog will automatically want to jump off and could damage its spine if the back strap is still attached. Conversely, make sure your dog can not slip its back legs off the table when the neck strap is attached as it could break its neck. It is important to have a hand on the dog at all times when grooming as it can be unpredictable when a dog is going to suddenly move when cutting or moving, and injury can easily result. Dogs are opportunists and will certainly take any opportunity to move or jump when you least expect it.

Preparation for bathing or grooming gives the owner the opportunity to look over the coat and skin for signs of abnormalities including parasites, injury, warts, skin conditions or bruising. It is important to do this examination as it could affect which products you will use on the dog for bathing and even whether you would want to bath the dog at all. The dog should firstly be brushed with a slicker brush selected for firmness and size for that particular dog. Any mats should be tackled with a de-matting tool and then combed to remove any little pieces of knotted hair.

Grooming out should be done in a methodical manner, working from one area to the next. When one section is knot-free, move on to the next in order. This way you do not miss any parts of the coat. The usual places for a dog to be matted are the heels, under the armpits, behind the ears, under the tail and between the toes. Pay special attention to these areas when grooming and shampooing. These are areas that, if left, can cause sores and irritation. Usually if a dog has a mat on one side it will have a corresponding one on the other.

If there are mats that are not going to be seen, for example on the insides of the legs, it may be kinder to remove these by clipping out with a #7F blade if possible rather than de-matting them, so that the dog is not distressed by tugging at the knot. If you come across a difficult, stubborn knot that is not a solid clump, you can use your thinning scissors underneath it and make a few cuts, then use your slicker to brush the knot out. This saves a bit of hair rather than having a missing section caused by clipping out. Small mats or tangles can be removed by using a de-matter in short strokes, working from the ends of the hair towards the roots as you de-mat a section at a time; this allows the hair that is being dealt with to be groomed into knot-free hair.

If the dog is excessively dirty, they will need to be bathed before brushing as the hair will just break if there is a lot of mud or dirt on it. If you are going to do a trim that involves a lot of hair being clipped off, it is more sensible to remove this prior to bathing so that you do not have to bath and dry hair you are going to clip off. This will cut down on drying time and, of course, electricity costs. It is quite important that you get your clipper lines reasonably accurate though when doing this so that you are not trying to blend higher on one side than the other. A tail ideally should not be clipped off unless it is really matted and grooming it out is uncomfortable for the dog. It might be a good idea to clip the dog's nails at this point too as, if they happen to get nicked, it is easy to wash any blood off the foot in the bath.

It is certainly worthwhile being particular in your preparation for bathing as it gives you a better result of the final cleanliness and finish when drying.

Choosing Products

For most breeds, getting a dog ready to start bathing consists of examination of the coat and skin and removing tangles or mats. The type and condition of the coat affects how we proceed with the task, for example if the dog is required to have a wiry-type coat, a conditioning shampoo will make the coat too soft. There are so many shampoos available to enable owners to choose a suitable one for their dog. Long silky coats often benefit from the use of conditioner after the shampooing process to keep the hair shaft flat and smooth.

Five Different Types of Coat

The first of these is the smooth type. This is the flat coat that lies close to the body with no length and also has a short undercoat, for example found on Labradors, Beagles and German Short-Haired Pointers. Usually a medicated or de-shedding shampoo is suitable for these.

The next is the double coat. This type of coat has a thick undercoat and longer, silky topcoat. Examples of this type are the Border Collie, Newfoundland and Rough Collie. Again, a medicated, tea-tree or de-shedding shampoo will be good on these coats.

Wire coats have a layer of undercoat and a rough top layer. Examples of breeds with this coat type are the Border Terrier, Scottish Terrier, Wire-Haired Dachshund and Italian Spinone. When these dogs are bathed, it is better to use a shampoo for wire or coarse coats.

Wool coats are softer with mostly undercoat and hardly any topcoat. This type of coat is found on Poodles, Poodle crosses and Bichons. An appropriate shampoo specially formulated for wool coats would be a good choice and these are readily available. Sometimes a whitening shampoo can be used on light- or white-coloured dogs. Surprisingly, these are usually blue or purple in colour.

Last, the silky coat is long and fine with quite a delicate look to it. Examples of breeds with this type of coat are Cocker Spaniels, Irish Setters, Yorkshire Terriers and all of the Setters. These coats need lots of conditioning so choose a shampoo that will provide this rather than just cleaning. I would always use a conditioner as well on this type of coat.

Coat Condition

Another thing to consider is the condition of the coat. Does it look dull, patchy, staring, and does the skin look scurfy, red, irritated, itchy or greasy? All of these things can affect how and which product needs to be used when bathing. A nourishing shampoo is useful when the coat is damaged and looks dull but, sometimes, it is necessary to think about the internal reasons for this problem. Does the dog need to be wormed, is the nutrition adequate or has the dog been poorly recently or had pups? All of these things can affect the quality of the coat.

As mentioned in Chapter 4, there are a lot of excellent supplements available from your vet or online that are specifically developed for the skin and coat. Most will contain vitamins and minerals such as zinc, which is

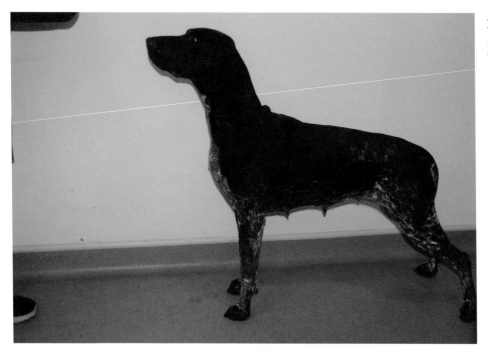

A very popular Gundog that does not need too much grooming to look good.

A lot of grooming is required with this member of the Collie family. They have a massive coat to protect them when working.

This breed is a member of the multitasking hunt, point and retrieve section of the Gundog group.

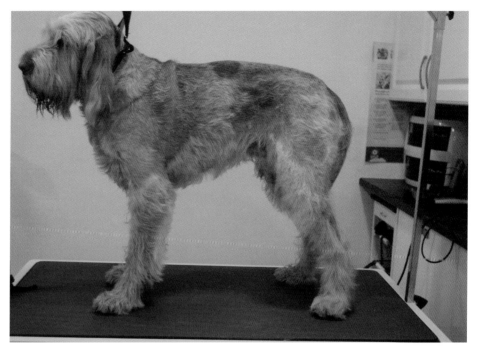

Some Poodles can have their hair left to grow into long ringlets. In the past, they could reach as long as three feet in length.

English Setters are often the biggest clown of the Setter family.

very important to the function of the skin. A nutritious diet is so important to the health of a dog's coat and skin, and no amount of products that you apply is going to help the quality of the hair if the dog is not being nourished internally. All the systems affecting the skin and coat are dependent on receiving the correct nutrition to be effective and show the health on the outside.

A staring coat often signifies a worm problem or underlying illness and this can be easily remedied by visiting your vet who, after an examination to ensure there is nothing amiss, can give you one of the great products available to rectify the problem. Worms extract the goodness from the dog's blood and the nutrients go to the worms instead of the dog, therefore the poor dog suffers. Sometimes a dog's skin will be very scurfy due to excess shedding of the top layers of the skin. A medicated shampoo can often help resolve this but needs to be used regularly to get it under control.

If a dog has an irritated skin you need to use a gentle shampoo such as oatmeal or a pure, non-perfumed one. Many dogs have allergies and cannot tolerate perfumed products or certain ingredients. Sometimes it is trial and error to find out which one can be used to bath your dog to avoid irritation and scratching, as this can become a habit if not nipped in the bud. When a dog has had pups, sometimes the nutrition goes from the bitch to the new babies and so she suffers herself. This is another time that a supplement can be of value and improve the coat massively. Often, after a litter, a bitch will shed her coat before growing a beautiful new outfit in a few months.

In some instances, if the coat is not too thick or matted, you can bath your dog first before clipping as the advantage of this is that it is not as detrimental to your blades and it is easier to clip a clean coat; although, in many cases, less hair to wash is advantageous as it is easier to make sure all areas are attended to properly.

Types of Shampoo

Most shampoos are composed of some sort of detergent. Detergents disperse fat molecules thereby releasing dirt and grease from the coat. As fat is sticky, it is difficult to get any debris from the coat or skin when this is present. There are several ingredients included in varying amounts in shampoo, depending on what the product is required to do. The main ingredient in shampoo is actually water. Shampoo might need to be chosen to nourish the coat, remove parasites, bacteria or fungi, soothe irritated skin, enhance the colour of the coat or improve the texture of the coat. The choice of shampoo is therefore important to achieve a final appearance to your liking and also to avoid changing a coat or skin that is susceptible to damage. The following are a few examples of shampoos that are easily available from pet stores, grooming supply companies or veterinary practices.

Medicated (including tea-tree-type shampoos) – Suitable for clearing up and minor skin problems, especially scurfy coats. This type of shampoo should be used on a regular basis.

Oatmeal – Suitable for sensitive skins or skins that need soothing.

Puppy shampoo – Non-stinging and gentle on the skin. A mild formulation. Should not cause any stinging to the eyes.

Antiparasitic – These are specifically for killing parasites on the skin. These can include fleas, ticks, lice and mites. Fungal infections can also be treated.

Hypoallergenic – This is especially blended to reduce the risk of a sensitive dog having a reaction to the ingredients. These will be successful if the missing ingredient was the one causing the problem; however, it might have been one still in the product, although great care is taken to remove the main culprits.

Colour enhancing – These shampoos can be red, black, brown, blue, purple or silver. Interestingly, the blue and purple shampoos are used on white coats as they have optical enhancers that make the coat appear much clearer and brighter.

These are just a few of the many, many shampoos available to buy. The only one not available in pet stores is a veterinary shampoo specially targeted towards the particular dog's health problem. These should never be used on another dog. Always dilute the shampoo according to the directions on the back of the bottle for optimum results and keep away from other animals and children.

Conditioners

There are many different types of conditioners and these are products that are manufactured to flatten down the hair shaft and keep it smooth. When many hairs come into contact with each other, they start to intertwine and become entangled, forming knots and eventually mats. Owners often ask what de-tangling sprays to use to get the mats out of their dog's coat. Often the mats are too far gone to be removed by using a product on its own. The best idea is to use the sprays to prevent the knots forming in the first place. If you think of flattening down the hairs so that they are straight and parallel to each other, they are less likely to catch and become knotted. General grooming with a brush and comb does this too and so keeps them in line. This is why it is important to groom your dog on a regular schedule.

Some conditioners are made to be applied to the washed coat and left in, while others will be allowed to sit on the coat for a specific amount of time and then rinsed off. There are oils too that can be used, which are warmed in hot water and then applied to a wet coat and finally shampooed off. Check how to use the one you have chosen by following the instructions on the product packaging. Using a conditioner after bathing will coat the hair with substances, sometimes silicon, to keep the hair shaft smooth to prevent tangling and knotting in a long coat, making it easy for a comb to glide freely through. Some conditioners are made to nourish the coat where the hair may be brittle or dry; again this repairs the ends of the hair by bringing all the barbs together and making them flat and smooth. You can apply this type by putting it onto a dry coat, either in a cream form or by a spray, and brushing it through the coat.

Shampooing

When your dog is securely placed in the bath and the shampoo correctly diluted to the manufacturer's guidelines, as per the label on the bottle, you can begin to apply it to the dog. I usually make up my shampoo in a basin or graded bottle that gives you the dilutions and amount of

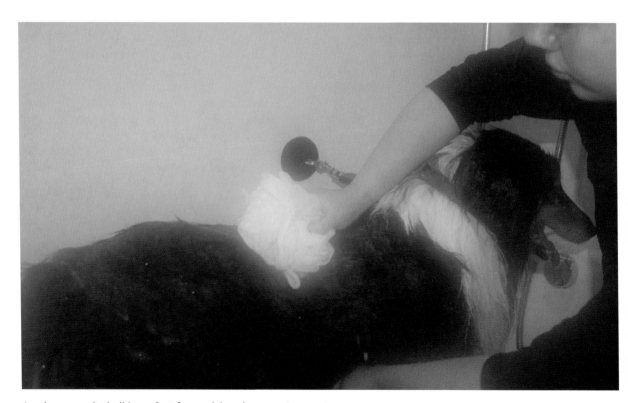

A nylon scrunchy ball is perfect for applying shampoo to a coat.

shampoo to go into it. These are available from grooming retailers. Apply the shampoo from the bottle or with a scrunchy net ball that is used in the shower for humans. Put the shampoo on to cover the whole of the dog and then, using your hands, rub it thoroughly throughout the coat, making sure the armpits, heels, under the tail, under and inside the ears and the feet are absolutely scrubbed clean. These areas are often missed when bathing a dog and, in fact, most people put neat shampoo on the dog's back and attempt to spread it down the body, unsuccessfully leaving the extremities dirty.

In a heavily coated breed it will be necessary to lift the entire coat up to ensure the water has penetrated the under layers and then do the same with the shampoo application. Once you have applied the shampoo, use your hands and fingertips to get the shampoo rubbed well into all areas of the body, tail and legs. Make sure you wash between the toes and under the pads of the dog's feet too. Lip folds should be washed as well. When this has been completed, rinse thoroughly, making sure that all the water is running clear with no soap residue left anywhere on the coat.

I usually wash the face separately from the body by either using a non-irritating, general-use product or a shampoo specifically made for washing faces. This is formulated to prevent eyes being affected by any ingredient that is liable to cause them to sting. In any case, care must be taken around the eye area when washing by holding your hands over the eye area. You must also still ensure that all of the head and surrounding area is thoroughly washed and clean.

The other part of the head that needs special care is around the ears. You do not want any water running into the ear canal; this can be avoided by holding your thumb on the canal when washing. Lack of care here could cause ear infections or inner ear problems that could affect the balance of the dog. The most common part of the head area to be missed is the lip folds. This is where a lot of debris from food can accumulate, especially in dogs who have pendulous lips. Gently pull the lower lip back and wash any folds that are present to remove stale food or saliva. Check that there is no redness or soreness here as often dogs can get dermatitis in this area too.

In breeds such as Pugs or Shar Peis, there may be wrinkles on the head that need to be attended to as well. When bathing these dogs, gently pull the skin back to flatten out the wrinkles so that the inside of them is washed and cleaned too. It is also very important when it comes to drying these areas that they are done thoroughly and not left wet. Once the dog has been well washed and you are rinsing, just check there are no areas of sliminess anywhere on the dog. This could indicate soap is still on the skin or coat and this may cause dermatitis if not removed and left to dry.

Drying the Coat

After the bathing process has been completed, you have a choice as to how you are now going to remove the water from the coat. The most efficient way is the use of a blaster to force excess water off the coat using high-velocity power drying. This also loosens the roots of the coat and makes it more open and therefore easier to dry. In a double-coated breed, a blaster also helps to remove excess undercoat and dead coat more easily than brushing or combing and with much less discomfort to the dog.

Most dogs are comfortable with being blasted; however, I would thoroughly recommend the use of an 'ear protector' that fits over the ears and head area to lessen the noise of the dryer or blaster. These come in various sizes to fit most breeds and are elasticated and very easy to fit. They can also be used where a dog is ear sensitive when having the rest of the body dried and often have a calming effect too.

There are certain times that I would never blast a dog, one of which is when I have a young puppy. Their journey through the grooming experience should be as calm as possible at the start and anything that may make them fearful of the process should be avoided at all costs. The blaster can be introduced slowly as time goes on so that they are not overwhelmed by too many new experiences at one time. If a dog is old or has epilepsy or heart problems, I would not blast them either.

There are some breeds where a blaster is really an essential piece of equipment to make grooming them an easier chore and these are the double-coated breeds such as Newfoundlands, Samoyeds, Border Collies and Rough Collies. It can be a long and tedious job to try to dry such a dense coat without the use of a blaster. Never blast around the head area of any dog or indeed the anus, as this could potentially cause damage to the area.

When a dog gets older, its senses can become much more sensitive and sometimes you will notice that your

You can see how the powerful blast of air has exposed a skin problem here.

dog has become more reluctant when being blasted, even though it has not had an adverse reaction in previous years. At this point, I would not proceed to blast the old dog, as often they will end up having a hysterical episode and are very frightened and panicky about the whole thing. It is kinder to compromise your groom a little at this stage of a dog's life and let it be groomed in its own comfort zone rather than force the oldie to have a perfect groom when it is not up to the procedure any more. It is also a good idea, depending on the type of coat and breed, to bath one day and groom another, thereby splitting the time the old dog needs to be on the table.

In a very old dog I would also have a trim as short as possible if this was the case. I would clip off the first day and bath the next – then you do not have any amount of excess hair to dry for a long time. I would not blast

a blind dog either as they may be very frightened when they cannot see what is going on and can only hear the noise of the blaster.

If you are using the blasting method and you have blasted the dog thoroughly, take a towel and dry the feet, tail and head. You should not be able to squeeze any water out of these parts by the time you are leaving the bath. Just a few points about blasters: they should always be plugged in at least 3ft (1m) away from the bath for safety; make sure you keep the filter part clear of hair to avoid overheating to let the blaster work properly; have a residual-current device (RCD) on the plug to prevent accidents.

This is a very important part of the grooming process as a dog that is dried correctly is much easier to style and a better finish can be achieved. After blasting, a stand dryer is the usual type to be used for general

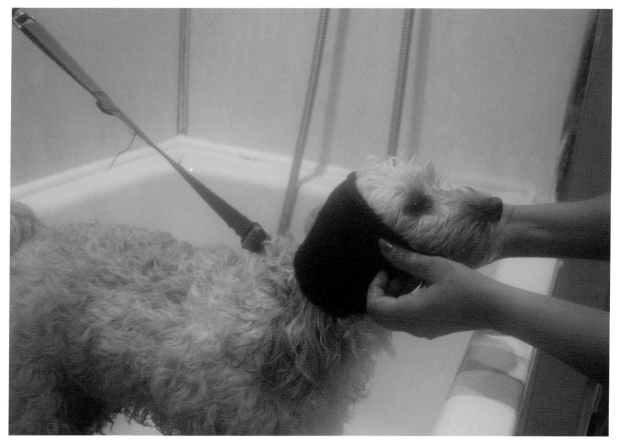

This dog has snuggly fitting ear protection that stops air getting into the ears and lowers the volume of the blaster.

drying. Natural coats should always be dried by blowing the coat down so that it lies flat on the body. The dryer should never be blowing the coat so that it is fluffing up and should be aimed from the head direction towards the tail. Sometimes, if the dog has a thin coat, it will be better to use a comb rather than a slicker brush here to prevent brush burn occurring, especially over the bony areas of the body and legs. Drop coats (also known as full coats; *see* Chapter 9), like Lhasa Apsos, Yorkies and so on, can also be dried in this fashion. Sometimes static can be a problem when drying some coats. If this is the case, an anti-static spray can be used during the procedure.

When drying double coats, aim the dryer onto a section of the coat and, using a wide-toothed comb, work from the epicentre of the area and comb from there. Never blow the coat upwards and then brush downwards against the way that it is blowing as this will be uncomfortable for the dog and ineffective in drying the roots.

In wool coats it is only possible to get a good scissor finish if we have got the coat to stand out as straight from the body as possible. This technique is called 'fluff drying'. It means stretching the coat outwards while running the dryer along the length of the hair. The most important thing to remember when doing this technique is to only dry the coat in sections and to do that thoroughly so that it is not left damp. Be careful too that your dryer is not inadvertently drying the opposite leg. If this happens, the coat will be very curly and will need to be wetted down with a spray bottle of water and re-dried. In all coats, check the heels, under the ears and also the underside of the tail as this is commonly missed when drying. This is also an area that often has a lot of knots so brush and comb through carefully.

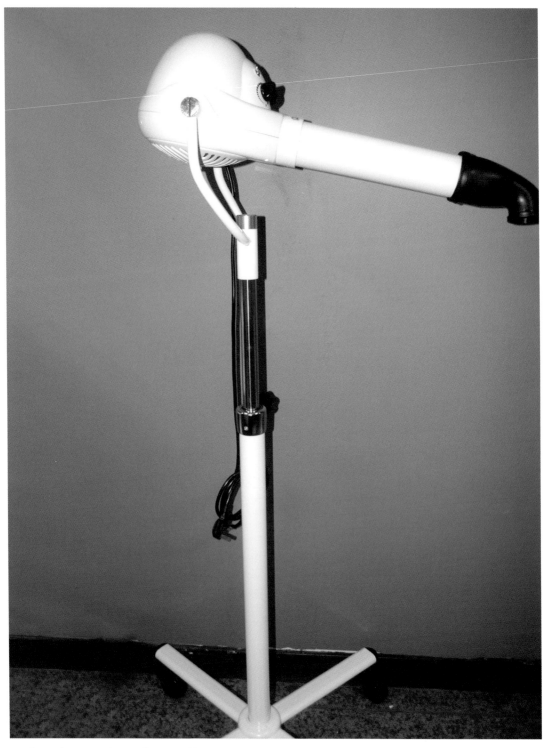

Finishing dryers can be used to reveal knots when grooming out as well as for doing the final dry on a dog. Ensure you keep the filters clean at all times.

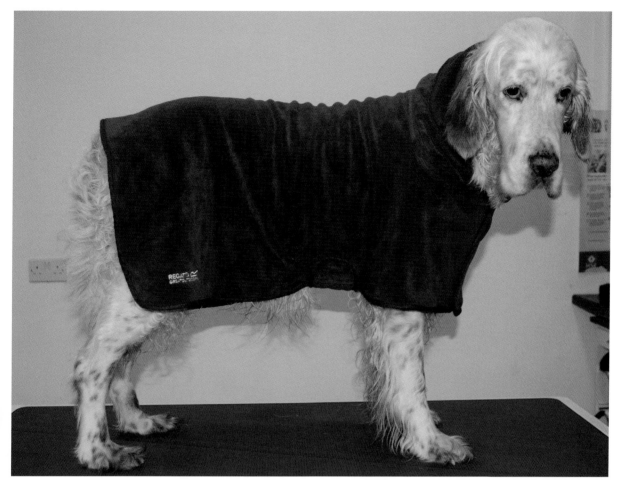

This is a good way to dry off your dog after exercising in wet weather or for flattening down the coat of a show dog.

With wire-coated dogs there is always a debate about when or why to bath them. I find that the coat strips much more easily when it is dirty as the grip is better. If I do want to wash the dog, I would bath it about two weeks prior to stripping or two weeks after. I find that the coat is a little too fluffy if bathed at the same time. I always use a medicated shampoo or one specifically formulated for wire coats.

In some breeds, for example Setters, it is possible to assist with the drying process by using a drying coat. This is a stretchy coat that is clipped quite tightly round the body to flatten the coat after the majority of the dampness has been removed but the coat is not totally dry. This can be left on your dog for the whole day but always remove before leaving the dog during the night or if you are going out. The drying coat can be used on most of the silky coated Gundogs with great results, especially if the coat is really curly or unruly. Previously we used to use a really thick towel at a size appropriate for the dog. This was pinned tightly at the chest, under the belly and under the tail. It gave a beautiful finish and was fixed with nappy pins that had to be secure in case they opened. Nowadays, we are lucky to have the specialized drying coats to do the same thing. One thing to be careful about when using the coats is to comb the hair with the growth and keep the hair totally flat when putting the coat on and when taking it off; otherwise you will pull the hair back up against the growth, causing it to stick up.

As you can see, the bathing and drying process is really important to the successful grooming of a dog and it is worthwhile doing it thoroughly for the optimum finish.

CHAPTER 6

Grooming Out

Grooming Out and De-Matting

Grooming out is a process that removes any matted or tangled coat prior to styling or bathing. It also helps to remove some of the dirt and debris from the coat. The tools vary, from slicker brushes and combs to de-matting tools, rakes or coat kings. Each has its own use and advantages and disadvantages for different coat textures or conditions. Be very careful when grooming if your dog has any form of skin problem, as brushing or combing may spread the problem to another area or might injure the skin if it is a bit fragile. The process of using your slicker brush should be short, quick strokes and not a long drawn-out one. If you follow the correct method, it will enable you to tease the coat out rather than drag it and it will groom through more easily. Always make sure your brush is suitable for the length and texture of the coat you are brushing and the pins are of the appropriate stiffness (*see* Chapter 2).

Begin by brushing a section of hair from the tips and working towards the skin each time. If it is a longer-haired dog you could pin the rest up so that it makes it easier for you to see the section you are dealing with at the time. Once you have brushed through the coat, you can comb it by using a double-sided comb. Use the wider side first, then the narrower side to make sure you have no knots or tangles left in the coat. The comb must be able to be brought right through from the skin.

Large clips are best for holding the hair up effectively. Grooming layer by layer prevents any parts being missed.

OPPOSITE: Clipping a wire-coated breed may be necessary if they have been neutered as it makes the coat soft.

Often an owner will put a comb into the coat and, when it gets stuck, take it out and comb nearer the ends of the hair, thereby missing the knotted area. When the dog arrives at the groomer, it looks lovely on the outside but when the coat is lifted up the undercoat is matted. The owners rightly insist they have been brushing the dog regularly, and are shocked when you have to tell them it is matted.

A good way to find mats in your dog is to use your hair-dryer while you are brushing through the coat. This will reveal the matted areas more easily, as it will blow away the outer hair to show you the undercoat, which is where most of the mats will be. If you bath a dog with mats it will become very clear where they are when it is wet, as they will appear as clumpy areas of thick impenetrable hair, which will be obvious from any areas free of knots. As mentioned in Chapter 5, it is usually much better to

This is a good general-purpose comb with long teeth that gets right to the roots of the longer-hair types.

get rid of mats prior to bathing by clipping them out if they are very big, and if the gap left is not going to be seen, as long as it will not compromise the overall style of the groom.

You can do this by splitting the mats up and grooming them out using a de-matter. These de-matters must be used very carefully as they consist of rows of blades that will slice through the mat, making it more manageable to deal with. As with using a slicker brush, begin at the ends of the hair; then, using your other hand to protect the skin, make short, sharp strokes to split up that area. Continue in this manner all the way up the hair shaft until you get to the skin. Because you have got the area below the first layer knot free it should be easy to de-mat the rest, as there will be nothing for the hair to get tangled in now. You can use a de-tangling spray of your choice while doing this. Keep the dryer on at a low position to help with blowing away the hair that has been removed from the mat.

If you decide that the mat is too big, take your clippers with a #7F blade and, making sure you are clipping under the mat and not through the clump of hair, remove it. If you are not clipping under the mat correctly it will be very difficult for the blade to cut through it and it will stick. Never force the blade through but take it back out and reposition it under the mat. Go under and remove the matted area in short strokes. Try to make sure you avoid any long hair that will be needed for the actual style and shape of the dog, as if too much has to be removed on the outer profile of the dog, it may be necessary to clip off the whole dog and begin to grow it in again.

Structure of a Mat

In a dog that has not been groomed, the structure of hair is a main trunk with bristle-like parts of roughened keratin sticking out from the main area. Through normal action of exercise, playing or just generally moving about, these spikes start to move away from the main shaft and become intertwined around each other. They get stuck together, first forming a tangle but, as time goes on, the clump gets bigger and bigger and before you know it a mat has appeared. This is why regular grooming is important and all of the body areas need to be done thoroughly as, when left, mats can cause not only health problems but distress to the dog. I would like to identify at this point the main areas that are neglected when grooming and how to deal with them, and also parts that may be more difficult to deal with.

Problem Areas

Armpits

This part of the body can be very awkward to groom as it is tucked away in an area that is not easily seen, so a different approach will be required to deal with these. First, taking hold of the foreleg, ease it into a forward position. Make sure you never pull the dog's front leg to the side. Take your comb and position it upwards to point towards the body of the dog. If you start by putting it in this position you can then rotate your comb upwards and towards the front of the dog's body. You should be able to feel any knots in that area. There is also a hollow where the armpit sits that you should be able to feel, and it is important that this part is well groomed out. Once you have identified any problems in this area, go to the other leg and repeat the process on the inner armpit area.

With a little practice, any knots will be easily removed, thereby reducing any friction in that area. If you have to clip out mats here, it is much safer to use clippers than a pair of scissors, as there are no pointed parts to snip an area of skin. However, care must still be taken when using them. As you did for mat removal, work carefully, and just do a little stroke at a time. Be very aware of the small, thin area of skin on the back of the elbow when clipping here.

Pads

It is very important that a dog is comfortable when walking around and is free from any pain that can be caused by matted feet. Underneath the pads can have quite a lot of hair in some breeds, and in some really active breeds, the pads can become very caked with mud and mats can form. There are certain breeds of dog, for example Setters and Collies, that need the protection of some hair between the pads, but this does not need to be excessive and any mats must be removed by using the tips of your little scissors under the matted area and snipping as you go along. It can help to wash the feet first and try to loosen the clumps away from the skin and between the toes. In other breeds, like Poodles, if the hair is very

A correctly positioned leg for clipping out the inside of a foreleg.

matted, you can use your trimmers on a #30 setting to clip out the mats and debris. Because this has probably been uncomfortable for the dog for a little while, the skin may be a bit red when the matted hair is clipped out. Always wash this area thoroughly. You could apply a little soothing, antiseptic cream to the area. If your dog has mats between the toes, take your little foot scissors and, cutting from underneath the foot, snip away the knot bit by bit.

Ears

When grooming the dog's ears, you must remember that the skin can be quite fine here in a lot of breeds, so go gently with the slicker brush as you do not want to damage the leather or make it bleed. If you are grooming a breed that requires the hair on the ears to be removed, the biggest concern is the little fold at the inside back of the ear; it is really important that when you clip, you do so outwards to the edges and not down the edge of

A very hairy foot here, which can hide a multitude of problems when you remove the hair.

the ears. Miniature Schnauzers are particularly prone to having this part of the ear damaged when clipping, for some unknown reason.

You should always use trimmers when clipping off ears, as they are more forgiving and quieter than normal clippers. You can use a #10, #15 or #30 blade when clipping the ears, depending on the breed you are clipping and how short you actually want them to be. Begin at the base and clip downwards towards the tip. Afterwards, angle the blade outwards to clip towards the outer edge and come right off the edge. Turn the ears inside out and repeat the procedure, but be very sure you are careful around the flap. You can complete this by scissoring around the ear from base to tip.

Groin and Waist

It is a good idea to keep the groin area free from hair as it helps avoid the coat becoming wet with urine, especially in males. The easiest way to do this is by using a #10 or #7F blade on your regular clippers and getting the dog to stand up on its hind legs (only if it is able) by holding up the front paws. Doing this means it is much easier to see the nipples and the hair to be removed. Just proceed by clipping out the excess hair under the belly and any dirty or contaminated hair on the inside of the back legs. Around the vulva can be done as well, to avoid the dog

Be very aware where all of the parts of your scissors are at all times to avoid cutting the pad accidentally.

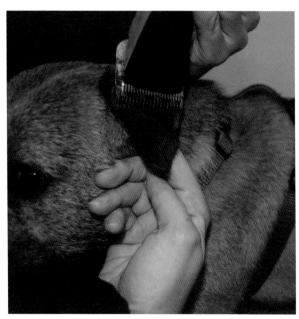

You have to be so careful when clipping ears as dogs are apt to shake their head when they are being groomed.

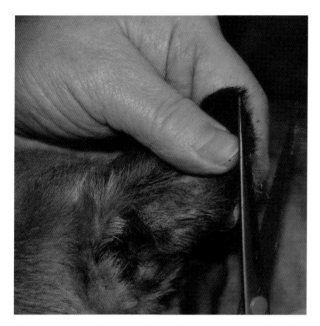

By using your nail as a guide, accidently shaving a slice of the edge will be avoided.

becoming smelly due to urine soaking the hair. When clipping the side of the dog, never clip sideways along the flap of skin at the waist. It is better to do this part by pulling the hair down from the body and watching where the skin starts. This is an area that can easily be cut with the wrong use of clippers, so easy does it and follow the correct direction.

Anal Area

I don't tend to use clippers around this area as it is very easy to catch the folds of skin with the blade. Instead, I use small foot scissors and pull the hair away from the body and snip the excess away with the points. Lift the hair up and away from the skin if possible to make it easier to get the tips of the scissors underneath. This area needs to be kept clean and free from hair for hygiene reasons.

Tail

The tail is a continuation of the spine, so you should remember when you are grooming it to keep the positioning comfortable for the dog. When grooming or trimming this part of the dog, hold the tail straight out from the body and groom as normal to the roots. Then repeat on the other side. Be particular about the hair directly under the root of the tail as this is often missed.

It is often tempting for people to hold the tail directly upwards and brush downwards to the underside of the root of the tail. This will almost certainly cause the dog discomfort, especially if there are any tangles there, as you are brushing against the growth of hair by doing this.

Clipping Off

Whether your dog is ill, the coat has become matted and is unmanageable or you just prefer not to have so much hair to groom (especially if your dog is very active and goes into water or bushes a lot), it is imperative that you have some guidance before attempting to clip the whole coat off. I usually use a #7F blade but you could use a #5F instead if you want it a little longer. A #7F is the most successful finish on dogs, especially if you are clipping off the legs too. It can be very difficult to leave the hair any longer if clipping off, especially if the coat is matted. I usually begin at the back of

Some dogs may itch after the groin is shaved so watch out for any irritation.

75

This is a very delicate area and needs to be treated so carefully when grooming.

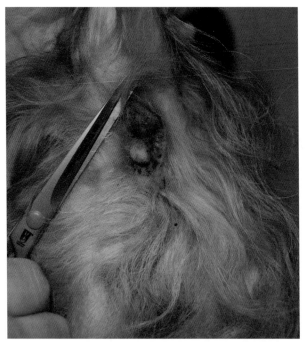

Make sure you keep this area clean at all times as it can attract flies that will lay their eggs there.

the head, keeping my clippers pointing downwards so that the blade is almost in contact with the skin. I then work my way in small strokes towards the base of the tail.

Step 1 – Start at the Adam's apple, which is just under the chin and can be felt as a small lump, and proceed down to between the front legs. If you are really particular about not seeing a few patches of closer-shaved hair, then use your thinning scissors over this part. This is caused by the hair growing in different directions here as, if you clip against the growth, it will always be shorter where there is a variation in the growth pattern.

Step 2 – Begin to clip from behind the ear downwards and right off the shoulder. When clipping the sides of the dog, do not clip straight down as this will cause lines that will be difficult to get rid of. Clip with your blade pointing almost across the side and never use the blades in reverse when you are clipping here.

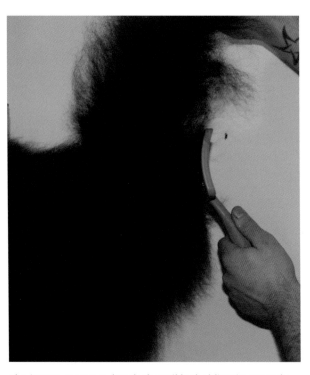

The incorrect way to brush the tail by holding it upwards.

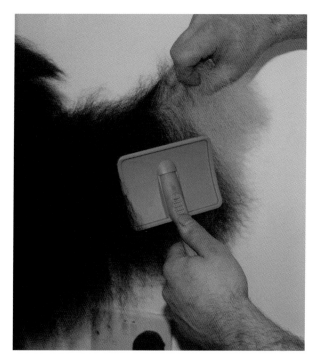

The correct position to ensure there is no discomfort for the dog.

Step 3 – Pull the hair down under the chest and abdomen as this will allow you to see where the skin or nipples are, and carefully remove all excess hair from this area.

Step 4 – The next step is to clip down the back leg, being very careful over the bony areas as they can easily be caught with the clippers. When clipping the inside of the back leg, gently lift the leg outwards, not upwards, with your table at a suitable height, and clip against the growth to remove the excess from the inside of the leg. Try to make sure you remove all the hair from around the genitals too.

Step 5 – Now on to the front leg. Lift the leg towards you and clip down the whole of the front of the leg and off the foot. Repeat the process on the outside of the front leg and at the back of it so that it is clean. Now comes the trickier part. Stand with the dog's front leg towards you and, holding the paw, begin to clip from the dew claw up against the growth, making sure that you are catching all of the excess hair that needs to be removed, including the armpit.

Step 6 – Start to tidy up your groom, as all shaved-off dogs will have the same natural shape of feet. They are shaped by trimming under the pads and pulling the excess hair up from between the toes, and thinning downwards if possible with thinning scissors to remove the excess hair. Never trim this hair across the way as it can result in unsightly lines across the top of the feet and may even graze or cut the knuckles. Finish the feet by trimming around them with your little foot scissors.

At this point, you will decide whether you are clipping the head or not. If you are clipping off the whole head, start at the eyebrows and work back over the head, being careful not to catch the edge of the ears with the blade. Work down the sides of the face, removing as much of the hair as possible with the growth. Very carefully clip from the middle of the eyes on the nose section, against the growth to enable the blade to catch the hair and avoid contact with the eye area. Remove the rest of the hair on

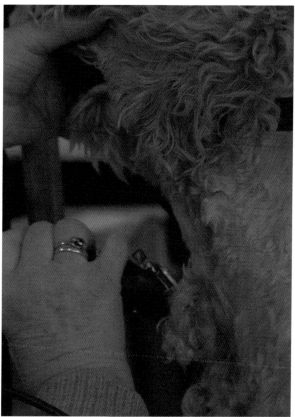

It is so important that you keep the chin up when clipping necks, as otherwise the blade may catch on the folds.

The more hair you remove, the easier it is to see the body area.

the muzzle at the sides in the same way until the face is clear of hair. Any stray hairs can be tidied up by carefully using the thinning scissors. Other face shapes will be dealt with in the breed styling section.

Unless the tail is really matted, this can be scissored and thinned to blend in with the rest of the coat. Remember to remove the long hairs at the end of the tail too. If you are in any doubt or worried about the safety of the dog, it is better to seek the services of a professional groomer for this type of groom and concentrate on keeping the dog in good condition in between grooms.

The following are a few different styles of head shapes that you can choose for your dog, especially if it is being clipped off and has no particular body styling.

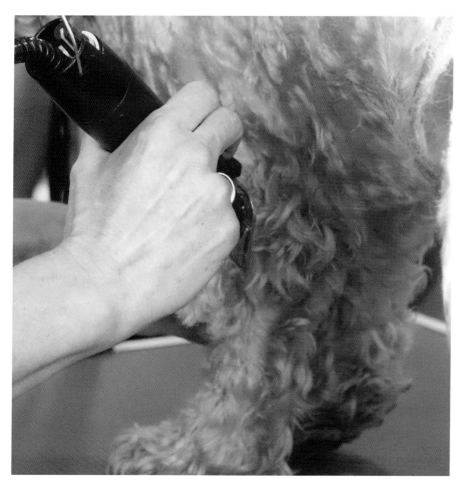

If you pull the hair outwards as you clip, you should be able to identify the curves of the back leg and where the joints are.

Head Shapes

Terrier Type

Clip from the back of the eyebrows, where you can feel the bony part, to the back of the skull with a #7F blade. Try to get this area as accurate as possible by clipping from the outside corner of the eye back to the neck, removing all the cheek hair, and continue under the chin in line with the corner of the mouth so that the line is even. With your thinning scissors, remove the hair from between the eyes and the top of the nose so that it is clean. Be careful not to remove any of the hair from the sides of the nose.

Carefully, remove the hair in the corner of the eyes by pulling it away from the skin to begin with and inserting the little points of your foot scissors or thinning scissors to remove the excess hair to clear the eyes. You

The terrier type head.

can decide if you want long or short eyebrows for your dog but, either way, clear the outside edge of the eye so that it is neat and tidy; then, using longer scissors, trim a triangular shape with the longest part coming straight forward from the inside of the eye. You can then trim the beard to whatever length you want and blend the area from the top of the nose down the side of the face as you wish.

Teddy Type

With this shape you can either have the hair on the ears left on or clipped off.

Step 1 – Begin by facing the dog towards you and using your comb as a guide when cutting or using a comb attachment clip; then, scissor the top of the head and down the cheeks. You may have to use your comb attachment and blade against the growth here to get a good enough finish. Then, using your thinning scissors, blend the hair on the sides of the face and trim to a suitable length to match the top of the head.

Step 2 – Hold the chin up and comb all the hair down thoroughly so there are definitely no knots. Using your longer scissors or chunkers, cut a line evenly across here so that there are no ends hanging down when combed.

Step 3 – Put the dog's head in the natural position again and lift up the top lip. Then carefully remove the dark, discoloured area below the canine tooth with your foot scissors.

Step 4 – Using your chunkers, thinners or scissors, begin to round the head by starting at the end of the nose and cutting upwards and round in a circle around the muzzle, removing any stray ends. When you are happy with the shape of the muzzle, continue up and around the head to blend the cheeks into the top of the head and the muzzle until you have the whole head rounded.

As an alternative to shaved ears, you can leave the hair long on the ears and carefully trim around the ends to even them up. Make sure you look at the dog from a distance on the ground when you are finished to ensure your ears are evenly trimmed and of a matching length.

You can do another variation on this trim by removing the cheeks and rounding the nose and head, but this time separate the moustache from the rest of the face by thinning in front of the eyes to form a band before the moustache begins.

Clean Heads

All Spaniels should have the hair on the whole head and face removed if they are being clipped, by clipping against the growth on the top of the head and sides of the cheeks or, in the case of Springers or working-type Cocker Spaniels, by using thinning scissors. Hold the head up completely as these dogs tend to have loose folds of skin that hang down and get caught with the blade if the head is not held high enough to stretch them out. Pull the bottom lip back to enable you to clip out the dirty bit in the lip fold and come straight off the chin. Make sure all clipped areas are blended into the next section of the dog so that there are no ridges.

As you can see, there are quite a few options for styling the heads even if the body has been clipped short. Really it is up to you and what you would like your dog to look like, and you can always vary the head style from time to time to give a different look.

Benefits of Keeping Your Dog Clean and Knot Free

The welfare of a dog is very important if you decide to have an animal as a pet or, indeed, for any other purpose. Their cleanliness and comfort all add to their quality of life with us. There are other reasons for looking after your dog through its time with us too, as animals can transmit infectious diseases like scabies, leptospirosis or ringworm to humans. If the coat is kept clean, any sign of a problem can be identified earlier and the chances of your family being infected are lessened. By doing a regular health check you will probably see signs of these diseases, thereby getting them treated quickly. If the coat or another part of the dog is smelly, it will not be a pleasant atmosphere to live in for you, your family or any guests that come to see you.

When a dog gets matted, the air does not get to the skin, therefore it is not able to breathe and can be a breeding place for parasites, bacteria or yeast infections. If the hair is matted it can also pull the skin, causing pain or discomfort to the dog. Sometimes a mat can form over an injury that is leaking fluid from the wound and then drying out. This becomes crusty and the hair soon tangles

Whiskers are often removed on Spaniels to make the face look clean.

around it. If mats are allowed to develop around the eyes they will join up, gluing the eyes closed, rendering the dog blind without actually being blind; however, potentially, because an infection can then occur, blindness may be a consequence if it is left for a while. The same thing can apply to the ears. Dogs like to be clean and get attention from people usually, but no one wants to pet a dirty, muddy or stinky animal that wants to get close to you or lie on your bed. Make everyone's life pleasant by looking after them well.

CHAPTER **7**

Natural Coats and Retrievers

Easy Styling

Natural-coated dogs are those whose hair parts in the centre of the back and falls naturally down the sides with no particularly obvious shaping. Some of them, including the giant breeds and Collies, will have a thick layer of hair called 'undercoat' underneath a silkier type of hair. Others, like Setters, will have much less undercoat but lots of silky hair. It is important when grooming all of them, however, that their coat lies reasonably flat at the end of the process, so the way it is dealt with is important to get a good result.

Essential pieces of equipment for most of these coats include a finishing dryer, a slicker, a double-sided and long-toothed comb, a de-matter, and a bristle brush for finishing and giving a shine. A blaster will be needed for the more heavy, thicker coated of these breeds, for example a Rough Collie. This allows the dead coat to be removed by 'power grooming', using a powerful jet of air for most of the groom. Like any other breeds, the preparation needs to be well done to allow the finished article to look good and therefore minimizing the risk of brush burn or distress to the dog by tugging and combing at the skin level. Ideally, the blaster should be variable in its settings to allow for nervous young dogs or extra thick coats.

A Rough Collie, for example will need maximum power to penetrate the coat and loosen the thick under-coat. The dog should be blasted prior to bathing and then again following this procedure. It is also very important to ensure that the coat is penetrated with water and the

shampoo mixture by lifting the coat up and saturating it to the skin, as many areas can be missed when the coat is so thick. After bathing, blast until the coat is almost dry as you will still get lots of dead coat being blown out of the dog. This will make the remainder of the drying procedure much easier.

When drying thinner types of natural coat, for example a Setter, it is important to blow the hair in the direction it is supposed to lie in and not against the growth, which would result in curly areas that stick up on the coat. Carefully blow the hair in the direction it is growing while combing the hair close to the body to achieve a very sleek finish. A comb will give a sleeker finish than a brush on this type of coat and using a pure bristle brush at the end will give a lovely shiny finish.

Double Coats

Double coats can be difficult for an owner to keep well due to the thickness of the undercoat. Therefore they can easily become very matted. It is quite difficult for a novice to groom them thoroughly enough without using efficient tools, equipment and techniques. Breeds such as German Shepherds, Collies, Huskies and Newfoundlands are in this group. This type of coat often gets brushed on top but the undercoat is left to build up into thick wadding, which then does not allow any air to get to the skin to keep it healthy. This often predisposes these dogs to skin problems.

OPPOSITE: A show champion Curly Coated Retriever sporting his unique type of coat. This coat is specialized for water retrieving.

Double-coated breeds should have an adequate amount of undercoat to complete the function for which they were bred; however, in a pet situation, they need a lot of time spent on grooming to keep it under control and healthy. A blaster is definitely an essential piece of equipment and so worth the investment if you are going to attempt to home groom. It is almost impossible to brush or comb to the skin without loosening off the undercoat first.

Place your dog on a table prior to bathing and blast as much as you possibly can until you feel that most of the loose hair has blown out and the rest loosened off. This can take quite a long time so do not be tempted to stop until most of the hair has come out. A word of warning here. It is advisable to wear a face mask when blasting as there is likely to be clouds of hair and dander flying round in the air. Goggles should be worn too. This is something to consider when grooming any dog, especially if you suffer from chest problems or asthma.

When doing this initial blast on double coats, make sure you pay particular attention to the chest area, under the belly and between the back legs, as these are areas often neglected. There is no need to brush the dog at this time as the blaster is doing the process for you. This is known as 'power grooming'. Ignore any little tangles that appear at the ends of the hair, as these can simply be brushed out at the end. Once you feel most of the coat has been loosened off, you can put the dog in the bath. If you try to do it before doing the first blasting stage, the water and shampoo will not get to the skin.

When you choose your shampoo for these breeds, usually a medicated or de-shedding one is suitable, unless the dog has a skin or coat problem. When bathing this type of dog, lift up the hair and ensure all of the undercoat is wet and shampooed right to the skin, as it is really easy to miss areas. Ideally, two shampoos should be done and rinsed well, ensuring no soap is left in the coat. Look to see that the water is running clear when you lift the coat up and rinse underneath. It should feel squeaky clean all over. Once the dog has been washed, I would use a good-quality conditioner, diluted following the directions on the bottle, to smooth down the hairs and make it easier to brush through. Rinse off the conditioner if the instructions indicate it, as some are designed to remain in the coat. This will also help to remove static from the coat.

At this point I would blast again thoroughly in the bath to remove the majority of the water and the rest of the loose hair. While the dog is still a little damp, I use a grooming spray containing silicon through the entire coat before beginning to dry with a stand dryer and long-toothed comb, rather than a slicker brush, to get to the roots as you dry. Only comb the area that is being blown by the dryer for efficient grooming. The blaster makes it simple to see the roots so combing from the centre outwards is much easier. Remember not to blow the hair upwards and then comb down.

Once you have worked your way through the entire coat, make sure you have groomed behind the ears and other thick areas, as you will possibly find knots and tangles here. If this is the case, carefully take thinning scissors and make a few snips under the mat and simply brush them out. If the mat is too bad you may have to resort to using clippers and a #7 blade to clip them out. You may come across other areas that are matted but unseen. These are usually between the back legs and the undercarriage. Neither of these two areas are going to be seen much so it is a lot kinder just to clip them out. This is also ideal if the dog constantly gets very dirty, and it will not be seen when the dog is on the ground so the style will not necessarily be compromised.

There are times when clipping panels out is very practical, especially if you have an incontinent bitch who constantly soaks the hair between her legs. If you remove the hair she will be so much more comfortable and much less smelly. Once this area has been washed you can also apply a barrier cream or nappy cream to prevent the urine burning her skin. Try to make sure you are clipping right to the skin but be very careful around the vulva. Never use scissors in this area and, if you are not confident, it is better to leave a little hair than cut the dog.

One thing that almost always a definite *no* is clipping the bodies of these double-coated dogs. People always think they are too hot and it would be less work when, in fact, it causes more problems as most of the time it grows back in thicker and more troublesome. Sometimes the opposite can happen too if the follicles are damaged: the coat does not grow in at all, especially around the rump area, and results in little stumps of occasional hairs. The skin can also look thickened and dark. This is known as coat funk. The only time I would clip off this type of coat would be if it was an old dog with a skin problem that had to be treated.

Now your dog is clean, and free from knots and dead coat, you can begin the trimming process.

Natural Feet

This type of foot is done on all of the aforementioned breeds of dogs and therefore the information given here is transferable to the trimming instructions of each one.

Step 1 – Begin by scissoring away any excess hair from under the pads prior to bathing and remove or loosen off any matted areas under the pads.

Step 2 – After bathing, and when the dog is perfectly dry, take your foot scissors again and remove the hair from under the pads as before and then remove the excess hair from around the edge of each pad, working under the foot. Always use appropriate scissors for the area you intend to cut. If you use large scissors for trimming feet you have more chance of cutting the dog as you will not be aware of the position of each part of the scissors during the process.

Step 3 – Holding the foot in your hand, pull all of the hair upwards from between the toes and begin to trim downwards or upwards only – *never* across the foot or you will end up with lines across the top of the foot and possibly take a scraping off the knuckle of the toes.

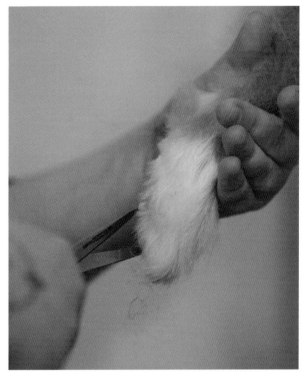

Never lift the leg up high when you are trimming pads. Raise your table instead.

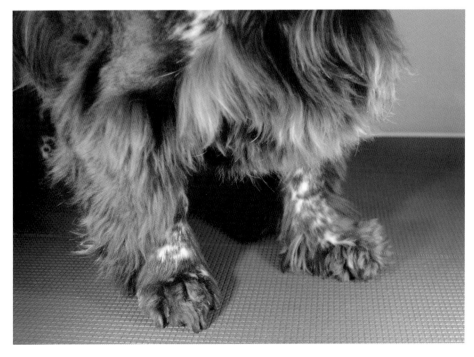

An example of a foot that has been cut across the way with scissors.

Step 4 – Finally, use your scissors at a 45-degree angle to lift any hair that is lying on the table by using the bottom blade to lift it to make it tidy.

This forms the basis for many of the following grooms, and, with a little practice, can transform hairy, unkempt feet that carry in much of the mud and dirt to our houses into beautiful tidy feet that will help with the health of your dog.

Retrievers

Golden Retriever

When the dog has been bathed and dried completely, card the coat using a rake or a finer comb to remove any remaining dead undercoat or loose hair so that the coat will lie as close to the skin as possible all over the body. When you are happy that there are no thick areas left, especially between the back legs, around the breeches, under the ears and the throat and neck areas, comb through the tail, ensuring that the comb can pass from the skin to the ends freely and without getting snagged.

Step 1 – I would usually begin with trimming the feet and therefore, following the instructions previously described, complete the natural feet on the dog. Once the feet have been trimmed to your satisfaction, take your thinning scissors and, pointing them downwards, remove the excess hair from the hock to the heel. Make sure you do not leave any hair sticking out from the actual heel. Take note that the dog only has hocks on the hind legs not the front.

Step 2 – At this point, you can now go on to the head and neck area. Lift up the ears and, using your thinning scissors, remove all the excess hair from underneath, especially if there are knots where people have been petting the dog. This can be taken close but be very careful that you know where the hair finishes and the skin begins.

A Golden Retriever bitch showing lack of coat after having a litter of puppies.

Step 3 – Looking at the dog in profile, we want to accentuate the throat and neck area, so this entails removing the longer hair from the chin to the top of the breastbone using thinning scissors only, never clippers. Sometimes there can be little flyaway areas that can be tidied using thinning scissors without going deep into the coat.

Step 4 – Remove any excess hair on the outside of the ears, but not digging in deeply, so that they appear smooth. There is a little fringe at the front top of the ear that folds back on itself; this can have a little fringing left on it (but not excessively) to soften the appearance. Finish by using thinners around the ear to tidy the edge, working from the base to the tip.

Step 5 – The next stage depends on how short or manageable you want your dog to be. At this stage we can shorten all of the feathering (longer fringing) from the legs and undercarriage of the dog. Begin at the back of the front legs and, using your longer straight scissors or thinners, whichever you feel more comfortable with, scissor downwards from the elbow direction and into the heel. Scissor a little wider at the elbow than at the heel. This can be adjusted to whatever length you require. Once you have done this, hold the leg forwards and tidy the line from the heel to the elbow, following the one that was cut previously.

Step 6 – The next area that can be shortened is the feathering of the undercarriage. So, standing at the side of the dog, use thinners or long straight scissors and trim from the groin towards the front of the dog and continuing between the front legs. This line should slope slightly. Just remember that you need to include all the hair in the middle of the underline. Please ensure that you hold the penis away from the cutting area on a male when you are scissoring this part to avoid accidents. The longest hair needs to be falling straight down from the breastbone.

Step 7 – Next, move around to the back of the dog and trim the thick hair of the breeches in a curved fashion to reach the top of the hock. Just ensure it is trimmed in an A-shape between the legs.

Step 8 – Lastly, hold the tail straight out from out from the body and measure it to where the bone reaches the hock. Then, leaving 1–2in (2.5–5cm) depending on how balanced it looks, hold the end of the bone and remove the excess hair with the thinning scissors after twisting the

hair around with your fingers. At the base of the tail where it meets the body, trim 1in (2.5cm) underneath to separate the body from the tail and scissor around the anus for hygiene purposes. Using straight scissors, remove the finer long hair that is under the tail from the tip to the base in a curved fashion. Make sure you hold the tail straight out and not upwards when cutting it. Ideally you would be trimming to the thicker, more dense part of the tail. Finally, you can apply a finishing spray to set the coat.

Curly Coated Retriever

This breed is not as popular as the Golden Retriever but it is important that, if you do buy one, the coat is treated properly so that the trademark of the breed, the tight curls, are preserved. This breed is not brushed or combed regularly, as this straightens the all-important curls. You will notice that there starts to be a loss of hair that is more than usual and the coat may become thick and dull. This is the time the coat needs to be raked out with a medium-width comb to remove all of the dead and discarded coat. Make sure you comb the breeches, under the ears and the neck and throat area with this comb until no more hair comes out. This usually happens a few times a year. Every dog is different but you will know when the coat begins to look really thick and dead at the roots, especially round the top of the back legs.

Once this hair is removed, it is time to get your dog into the bath. A medicated shampoo is ideal for this breed. Wet the coat thoroughly and apply diluted shampoo all over the body, legs, head and tail. Once this has been applied, use your fingertips only to massage the shampoo into the coat in a circular manner. You will find that there is quite a lot more of the loose hair that has attached to your fingers. Rinse this thoroughly and repeat the process.

Never rub or blast this coat, but use a thickly folded towel and press down onto the coat section by section to remove the excess water. When you have done this, take the dog from the bath and allow the dog to shake. At this point it is a good idea to walk the dog to allow more of the water to come off the body naturally. This is how a Curly Coated Retriever would get rid of it after water retrieving. The coat is designed to dry off very quickly due to the curls – air gets trapped and warms up, just like a cellular blanket or bubble wrap would work, and so prevents the dog from becoming chilled.

Once the dog is relatively dry, although it does not have to be totally dry, you can begin to scissor all over it to tidy

A super example of the tight curls of the Curly Coated Retriever.

the outline and give it a shape. No comb or brush is used when doing the scissoring or any other work from now on.

Step 1 – Using your long, straight scissors and keeping your hand evenly from the dog, begin to scissor off the tufts on the ends of the curls to make them crisp rather than fuzzy. Follow the shape of the body and remove untidy hair from the groin and undercarriage to give a clean appearance.

Step 2 – Remove most of the hair from underneath the tail and tidy the top to match the body. Do not take too much off on top.

Step 3 – Follow the instructions in the 'Natural Feet' section for completing the natural feet and tidy the hocks.

Step 4 – Scissor the head and ears, which should be short, and work around the edges neatly.

Step 5 – The back of all of the legs should be trimmed correspondingly to the rest of the groom to enhance the shape.

Step 6 – When the scissor work is done to your satisfaction, spray your dog with a fine spray of water to set the curl and, using your comb, turn the line on the top of the head over to emphasize the transition from flat to curl.

Do not be tempted to brush or comb again.

The ears should be small on this breed, so no excess hair should be left around them.

This breed has a good waterproof coat that repels the rain with hardly any penetration of the undercoat.

Labrador Retrievers

There is not usually a lot of trimming necessary in the Labrador Retriever but some grow a little more hair in areas that could be enhanced by tidying it up. The feet sometimes are a little hairier than normal and can benefit from trimming like a natural foot. Sometimes the undercarriage, between the hind legs and underneath the tail can be carefully trimmed with thinning scissors to neaten up the profile.

Bernese Mountain Dogs, Newfoundlands and Husky-Type Dogs

Newfoundlands have a natural fall of their coats but the main problem with grooming them is their size and their thick double coat. It is essential if you are going to own and maintain this type of dog that some investment in equipment is needed to do the grooming successfully. A table of suitable size, and that is sold as being capable of withstanding the weight of these dogs, is a must. The other piece of equipment that is needed for this breed and for Husky types is a very powerful blaster, which should be used regularly to keep the amount of dead undercoat

out of the coat. If this is not done, no air can possibly get to the skin and the lack of air contributes to infections of the skin and a particularly mouldy smell. The Newfoundland breed does tend to slobber a lot and they are often seen wearing a special bib to avoid wetting or discolouring the neck hair.

It is essential to ensure that these types of dogs are thoroughly bathed with a medicated or tea-tree shampoo to remove bacteria and dirt from the coat to keep them scrupulously clean. Be very particular when washing between their toes too. It is possible to remove hair from the belly area and also between the back legs with a #7 blade to help keep those areas from matting, getting particularly dirty and smelling. These types of dog do tend to lie around outside and accumulate a lot of mud and dirt and may also wander around in the rain. This can make them really difficult to clean quickly when you want to bring them into a house.

This type of breed can also have trimmed, natural feet, which is obviously going to make their maintenance and cleanliness in the house easier than wearing huge carpet slippers. The Newfoundland can be tidied up with the use of thinning scissors or chunkers under the neck and on the longer wispy hair and feathering. Be very careful if your Newfoundland lives outside as the coat can become

Newfoundland, Noah, sporting his own personalised bib to catch his slobbers.

a real mess, especially if walking about in the rain, as the coat on the back of the black dogs will become brown and brittle and be difficult to groom if left. If you have a black dog and it is out in the sun, the coat can get damaged by the ultra-violet (UV) rays and this too can turn a black coat brown on top, so avoid excesses of weather if you want to keep your dog in good condition. You can also buy UV sprays to reduce the problem.

It might be necessary to wash your dog's face on a daily basis to remove saliva and any eye discharge to prevent the whole face smelling. There are special face washes or scrubs that you can buy or antibacterial soap that can be used on dogs. Ensure this is thoroughly rinsed and dried, including the lip folds.

The tail can be trimmed like the scimitar shape of the Golden Retriever.

Smooth Coats

This type of dog is often bought as people sometimes don't want a breed that is going to require a lot of grooming. Some of the breeds in this category are Dalmatians, Smooth Jack Russell Terriers, Beagles, Pointers and the Weimaraner. While it is true that there are not going to be knots and tangles in this coat, they do take quite a lot of work to keep their coat from causing a problem in most homes due to the amount of shedding, especially if in a hot environment. It can be a never-ending chore to keep the tumbleweed of coat off your floors and carpets. The best solution to keep on top of the situation is to invest in appropriate grooming tools and products. There are excellent de-shedding shampoos available that can be extremely effective on reducing the problem. They will not prevent hair from falling out naturally but will efficiently remove the already cast hair that is just waiting to make its way onto your floor every time the dog shakes or walks about.

After using the blaster, try to blast the dog thoroughly as this will force loose hair out of the coat. You can also use a rubber brush when shampooing the dog to massage the coat and skin to loosen off any hair from the follicles that is almost ready to leave the body. Once the dog is thoroughly dried with a stand or hand dryer, get to work vigorously to expel the loose hair from the body and muscular areas by using the rubber brush. Continue on the head and legs as well but in a more gentle fashion.

Another super implement for removing loose hair is the blade rake. This should be used gently over all of the body until no more hair is shedding from the dog. There can be amazing amounts of hair that can be released from just one session. It is important to make sure you take as much as possible out around the thick breeches area and also under the ears. Some of these short-coated dogs sometimes grow an excessive amount of hair under their tail, belly and on the feet. This can be removed, if you require, through the use of thinning scissors, and the feet tidied up following the 'Natural Feet' instructions again. As a final finish, the whole dog can be sprayed with a coat gloss or finishing spray that will help to set the coat and stabilize casting for a short period.

A good grooming method for these breeds is to do what in horseman's terms is referred to as 'strapping'. This can be done by lightly slapping the muscular area with cupped hands, hand over hand. There needs to be a little bit of pressure used to stimulate the hair follicles, sebaceous glands, blood vessels and lymphatic system. This is all beneficial to the animal and is almost like a massage. The stimulation of the sebaceous glands will result in a glorious shine and it can all be finished off by polishing with a velvet or silk cloth if you have any lying around.

One of the smooth-coated breeds is the very popular Pug. These little dogs have quite a harsh coat that requires regular brushing with a bristle brush to keep it in good order. They need particular attention when being bathed as it is important that the wrinkles are well washed and definitely completely dried to avoid skin problems. If you take a cotton bud and run it between the wrinkles, this will help to make sure they are not damp or dirty. Make sure these little ones get their ears cleaned on a regular basis too. The Pug is notoriously stubborn about getting their nails trimmed so it may be necessary to leave that job to a groomer or vet. It is very important that you handle these little dogs carefully as they are prone to getting a prolapse of the eyeball. This is where the eye falls out of the socket. Therefore try to avoid pulling the skin back on the top of the head or restraining them by the neck skin. Care also needs to be taken when grooming to avoid the eyeball getting scratched, as the eye is quite rounded and prominent in front of the face.

CHAPTER 8

Hand Stripping

Wire Coats

In comparison to longer, softer-coated breeds, wire-coated ones are relatively easy to care for on your own. Regular brushing is an essential requirement to remove dead, loose coat that will be produced on a regular basis. The clearing out of this coat will make the colour brighter as well as making it much easier to strip. The basis of most hand-strip wire coats is that there are two layers to it, the topcoat and undercoat. The undercoat needs to be raked out regularly to remove the dead, dense hair to allow the topcoat to lie flat, improve the colour of the coat, make the skin healthier by allowing more air into it and enabling the breakthrough of the new topcoat to come in easier.

The undercoat is relatively soft compared to the topcoat, which is very harsh and wiry. The reason for undercoat in a dog is often to give the dog some warmth

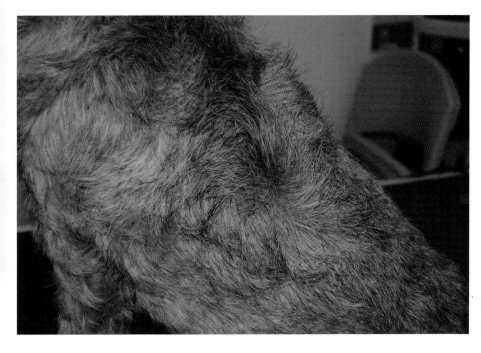

There is a super coat on this dog. This makes the task easier.

OPPOSITE: Overgrown Border Terrier just before his pamper session.

and to protect the skin to some degree, whereas the wiry topcoat gives the dog some waterproofing and dirt resistance because of the slippery, smooth surface of the hair shaft. Ideally, a wire-coated dog should always have some topcoat to assist with this desirable property. This is only possible if the coat is regularly maintained by what is known as 'rolling the coat', which is a more advanced technique.

There are two ways you can deal with these coats. One way is by removing all of the topcoat two or three times a year and leaving the undercoat. The harsh coat will eventually all grow back in, but will be all one length and will not fit closely to the body. Alternatively, the coat can have a small amount of topcoat removed on a much more regular basis and be left in several layers close to the body. This means that there is always some of the protective coat there at all times. It also means that the colour of the dog will be correct as the pigment that gives the dog its colour is focused on the topcoat. This is 'rolling the coat'.

Some breeds have different parts of the coat stripped at different times to enable some areas to be shorter than others. However, this is not necessary in a pet dog. The easiest of these breeds for the pet owner to keep is the Border Terrier. In this breed the stripping is best done all at the one time. With a little practice, the muscles in your hands, that so many people complain are sore when they begin the process, begin to get stronger and eventually do not ache like when you first began to hand strip.

There are a few tools that are useful for the hand-stripping process for wire-coated Border Terriers. The easiest possibly for beginners is the stripping stone. This is a product from lava that can be bought in different degrees of hardness and different colours – black/grey or white. These stones usually come as a block that can be cut down by inserting a comb into the centre and pressing down. These would usually be enough to cut into four sections to make a comfortable size for most hands. Obviously, if your hands are on the larger or smaller end of the scale, you will need to adjust your cut to suit.

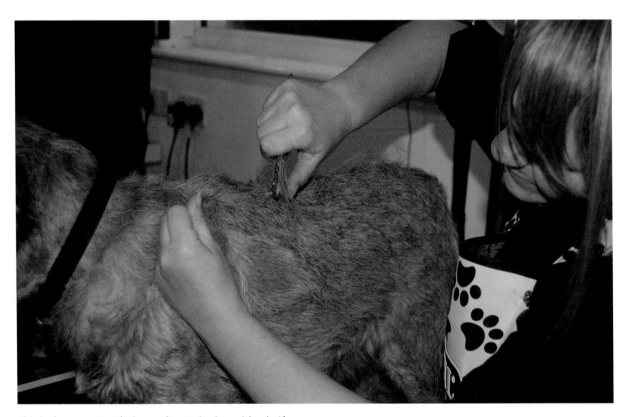

This is the correct technique when stripping with a knife.

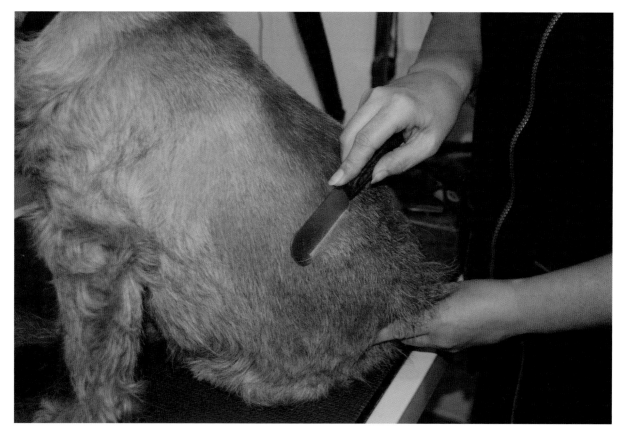

A carding knife must be used flat on the body to avoid cutting the coat.

Finger condoms can be useful for plucking individual or intricate parts of the dog when you want a more detailed amount of hair to be removed rather than a broad area. Other tools include stripping knives. These come in many variations and range from basic pet-quality knives to more professional types that cater for variations in area or the type of hair you are removing. These are really beneficial when grooming a hand-stripped coat and are used meticulously to get the desired finish on the dog over a length of time; for the average pet owner, however, they are only used to keep the dog tidy. A little practice is required to get the technique mastered but it can be achieved quite easily within a short time if you are eager to learn.

A carding knife is a flattish tool that is not sharp and is used to scrape out the dead undercoat. The hair must not be gripped between your thumb and the knife with this tool but, instead, lay the back of the knife on the

dog and scrape out the thickness of the coat gradually. You should only find soft undercoat when you do this. You will often find there is actually a lot of undercoat to come out when using this knife. A simple way of completing your hand strips, if your dog has a good coat, is by using the simple finger and thumb method (*see* 'The Stripping Method' section) and using some chalk. The main thing with hand stripping is to avoid doing the stripping in patches and becoming bored and leaving it to another day. The more you practise the technique the quicker you will get.

There is huge debate about whether to bath a dog to be hand stripped before, after or during the stripping procedure. I am 'old school' and prefer a dirty coat to work on most of the time. If I want to bath a Border Terrier, I do it well in advance, probably two or three weeks before stripping, or alternatively a couple of weeks after. This allows the coat and skin to settle down again and avoid irritation.

The Stripping Technique

Step 1 – Begin at the back of the skull and stretch the skin with one hand to form a flat surface. This technique prevents pinching of the skin and also eliminates any rolls of fat that may be around the neck area of the dog, allowing you to strip inside the folds. If you have a very heavy coat, you can use a coat king to remove excess bulky coat first to clear out lots of unwanted hair of both types, topcoat and undercoat.

Step 2 – If using your stripping stone, grip the topcoat only at the tips between your thumb and the stone while it is at a 45-degree angle to the body of the dog. Quickly, with a slight tug, draw the stone back towards you, making sure your thumb grips the hair on the stone firmly to prevent the caught hair sliding out. Try to repeat this procedure while gradually building up a rhythm that you can strip along to, a favourite upbeat song possibly. Make sure you are not pulling the hair upwards as this will be painful for the dog and also ensure that it is only the ends of the hair that are being gripped. This will keep your work even as you are doing it steadily. The objective, if you are stripping out the hair to begin the procedure, if you are doing a twice yearly strip down, is to only remove topcoat with the stone and not any undercoat. I find that most owners are not usually particular enough when doing the coat and leave too many stray ends, so try to remove all of the longer hairs by combing the hair in the opposite direction of growth and removing the longer hairs. In this instance, we will concentrate on the scenario of a full strip as this is what the majority of pet owners will be doing to their pet. When you grip the hair, pull backwards, never upwards as this twists the base of the hair as it comes out of the follicle. I usually work in a band from the stripped hair, in a methodical fashion, gradually to the base of the tail. As you remove the outer hair, you will notice the change of colour to a paler or darker shade than usual. Try to make sure you brush the coat up to expose any missed hair. There should be no wiry hairs remaining on the top of the undercoat now when you do this.

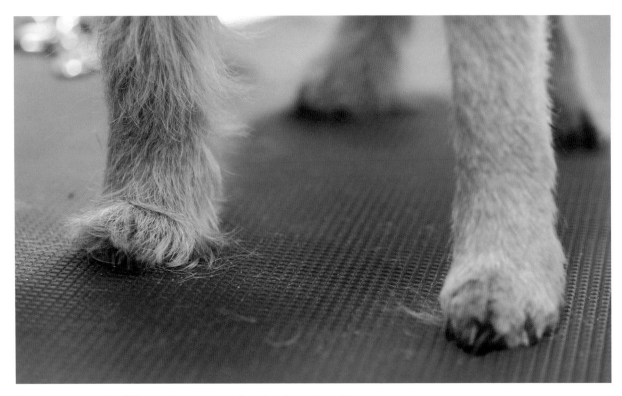

Here you can see the difference between a stripped and unstripped leg.

Border Terrier

This is probably the easiest and most common breed that we get to strip in a salon situation. There is very little styling required except for the head and face. Work all over the body as you have been doing and along the back and down the sides, continuing under the chest and throat to join the body between the front legs. The legs can sometimes be a little more difficult to strip with a stone so you may want to change to a knife. Be very particular that all the hair is removed from all of the leg and, again, keep brushing the hair against the growth to reveal any missed hair. Ensure that the tops of the feet are well stripped too.

As you progress there may be areas that are a little tender to strip and it is kindest to use thinning scissors very carefully on these areas by pulling the hair away from the skin first of all. These areas are mainly under the groin, under the tail and sometimes at the back of the hind legs. In all of these areas it is sensible to scissor using thinners to give a natural finish if stripping causes any discomfort whatsoever. This area is best left to the experts.

By holding the tail upwards, brush the hair against the growth and thin the underside quite closely, removing the excess hair. When this has been completed, strip the top of the tail by putting the dog into a sitting position and holding the base of the tail with your spare hand. This keeps the dog in place and makes it easier to strip the tail on top. Once you have stripped the top and sides of the tail, twist the hair on the end of the tail, ensuring there is enough protection over the bone at the end of the tail, and remove the excess hair using your thinning scissors once again. Doing this ensures that the end of the tail does not have an untidy flag when the dog moves.

Next we will turn our attention to the feet. Using your little foot scissors, remove excess hair from under the pads. Be very careful that you are paying attention to all areas of the scissors when cutting so that no part of the pad is cut. The next step is to pull the hair up between the pads towards the top of the foot and, using your thinners again, thin off the excess hair that sticks up between the toes – always upwards or downwards, never across. When this is done and the foot is on the table, tilt your little foot scissors so that the bottom blade is lifting up any hair that is lying on the table and scissor round the whole foot to make it neat and tidy. Cutting the nails prior to trimming feet often makes it much easier to get a neat finish around the foot.

When trimming feet, always check there are no hard knots between the pads.

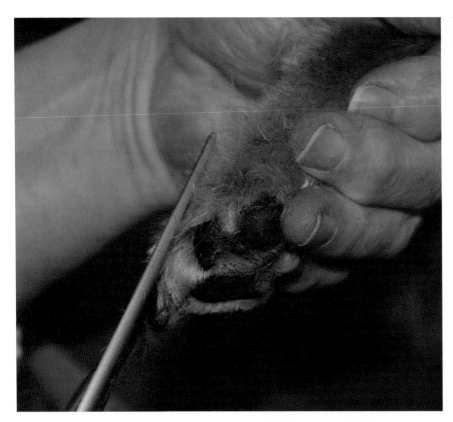

This method gives you a lovely natural foot shape that is suitable for many breeds.

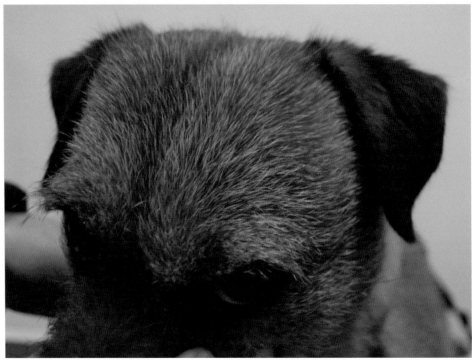

Head and cheek hair ready for removal, leaving he eyebrows for shaping.

When it comes to the head of the Border Terrier, this is the part that needs to be styled and takes a little bit more practice. Starting at the back of the eyebrows, strip backwards towards the body. Try to make the starting line very accurate if possible. Continue from the outside corner of the eye backwards, towards the body, and remove all of the cheek hair beginning at the outside corner of the eye, down to and ending at the corner of the mouth.

With your stripping stone or finger and thumb, strip all of the hair off the ear, making sure none can be brushed upwards. Holding the ear upwards, strip the hair on the edge of the ear to reveal a darker shade of hair around the edge. The hair between the eyes should be removed by using your finger and thumb to separate the two eyebrows. These are referred to as split eyebrows. If possible, remove the hair on the inside corner of the eye using the same method. If it is proving to be more difficult, carefully use the tips of your thinning scissors after pulling up the hair with your fingers so that it stands proud of the skin.

If you look carefully at the bottom jaw, you will notice that there may be a bit of discolouration on the hair below the canine tooth. The canine tooth is the large tooth at the side of the front teeth that is more pointed and longer than the others. Very carefully snip the discoloured area off with the tips of your scissors by pointing them upwards and holding the upper lip up off the bottom one.

Using your finger and thumb, pull the eyebrows to the outer corner and remove any excess hair from them. The eyebrows should not be too heavy and should frame the face without looking bulky. Then carefully comb down the chin hair by holding the dog by the hair that is nearest the lip. Use your thinning scissors to remove any excess hair from here so that this will form the lower part of your otter-shaped face. Lift the face towards you and comb the sides outwards to stand off the face. Begin to scissor the whole muzzle in a circle by scissoring up and around the moustache, forming a doughnut. If you comb all the hair forwards it may look untidy at the front of the face; if so, remove the dirty longer hairs with your thinning scissors.

When this is done you can then card the coat with the carding knife. This will remove the excess undercoat and clear the colour. All that is left to do now is wipe over the body with rinseless shampoo or a damp cloth to remove any loose hair remaining on the dog. Clean the ears as described in Chapter 3 and cut the nails remembering, the dew claw if the dog has one.

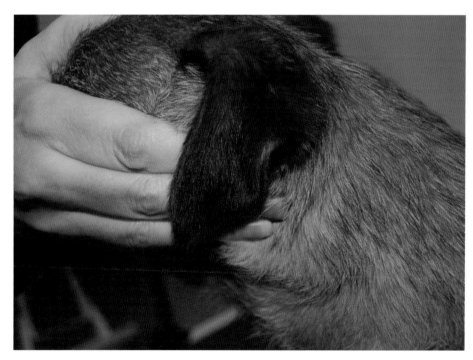

A lovely stripped ear showing off the neatly stripped edges.

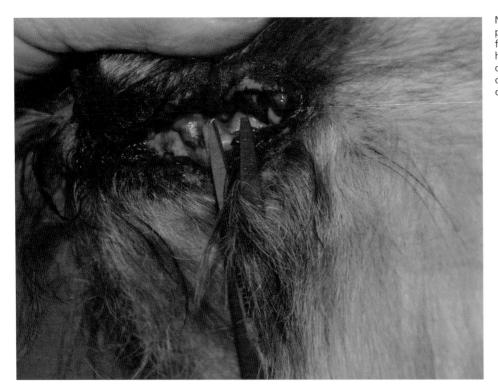

Notice the correct position of the scissors for removing this hair. The staining is caused by the action of chemicals in the saliva on the hair.

Just a little tidying at the front will improve the look but do not over-trim.

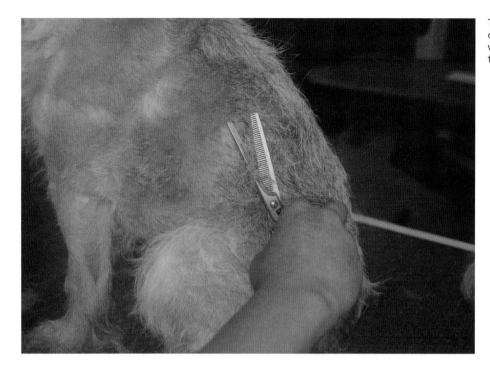

This is an alternative way of removing coat from a wire-coated breed – using thinning scissors.

If we want to go a step further and keep the dog 'in coat' we can learn to 'roll the coat' so that the hair is not taken right down to the undercoat but layers of topcoat remain, giving the dog the protection of always having some wire coat as an outer covering. I would recommend that you go to a bone fide grooming school to learn under supervision to begin with.

All of the wire body coats can be done in this fashion, the only difference often being the head and leg shape. There are occasions where it is not possible to strip the Terrier as it may be neutered, old or just have a poor coat. In these instances, it is better to use thinning scissors on them.

Silky Coats

These coats are totally different in nature from the wire coats that were described previously. This coat is composed of undercoat with a silkier topcoat rather than being wiry. From time to time, and when the dog is a puppy, there will be a fair amount of dead, discoloured coat which appears – especially in the case of darker-coloured dogs, it is often brown or fawn in colour. In liver and white Springer Spaniels or Irish Setters, the dead coat will have an orange appearance. This is not healthy coat and spoils the beautiful shiny coat that is hidden by this fluff. All of the coat will not necessarily be ready to come out when the dog is a puppy so, sometimes, you have to be patient and work on the coat regularly till, gradually, the beautiful shiny coat will start to show through. Topknots on Spaniels can be a bit stubborn sometimes but this coat will eventually lie flat with regular stripping and brushing, and a bit of work. Some coats are much easier to strip than others, especially Spaniels of working type who tend to have a finer texture of coat and not so much thick feathering or hair on the fronts of their legs.

The equipment that is useful in stripping these coats consists of finger condoms, banded combs, stripping stones, carding knives and good old finger and thumb. You can buy chalk specifically for stripping silky coats that can make gripping easier. Never use a stripping knife to strip this type of coat as it tends to cut it and spoil the silky topcoat. Using your finger and thumb with a finger condom is a very good method because you can target individual areas more accurately. Lift the hair up and gradually pull out the extra-long hair that is not

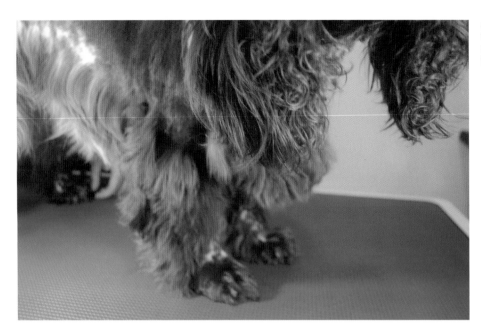

A big effort is needed here to make the leg smooth again by stripping or thinning the excess.

lying flat. Always strip towards the tail as this will be how the hair is coming out of the follicle and will not cause any discomfort to the dog when done in this manner. Never try to pull a big clump at a time. Just use the tips of your fingers to pull a few hairs at a time. Spaniels' and Setters' body coats can be done almost identically so I have described the process for both here.

Step 1 – Beginning at the head, strip the tufty hair that is on the skull. It makes it easier if you brush the hair against the direction of growth before stripping as it is easier to get a hold of the ends of the hair. Do not strip the hair next to the skin as this will result in a bald patch and be painful for the dog. Once you have stripped as much as you can, card the top of the head using the carding

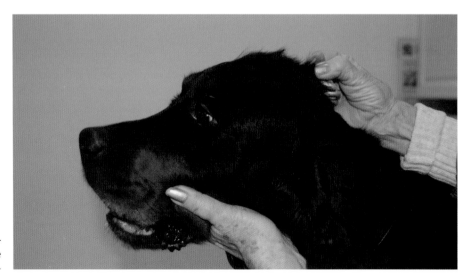

Gentle stripping of the hair on the skull needs to be done little and often.

knife to remove any extra fluff here. Some pet owners have a preference to leave a topknot on their Spaniels. This is usually only found on Irish Water Spaniels and American Cocker Spaniels but, if that is what you prefer, you can just do a little tidy up.

Step 2 – Continue down the back of the neck and into the shoulders and back. Work your way down the sides without removing much of the hair beyond the widest part of the ribcage unless it is a bit unruly. Strip around the shoulder and down the back leg to a little above the line of the hock. The coat will have a natural tendency to lie in place and, in some dogs, the coat will naturally fall from behind the leg towards the front in a downward fashion. This can add to the styling of the dog and overall natural appearance.

Step 3 – A banded comb can be used to successfully remove a lot of the dead coat. This in combination with finger-and-thumb stripping will give you the result you are looking for. Thinning scissors are usually necessary in trimming the throat and neck area of the Spaniel. You can follow the styling for the clipped Spaniel for the legs and feet.

Step 4 – Make sure you card the coat well, especially around the neck area where it may be necessary to thin a little if excessively bulky. Never do this on red-coloured dogs such as the Red Cocker Spaniel as it will change the colour if you cut into the darker red hair and expose the orangey undercoat. Stripping can be done down the front of the legs on Spaniels or Setters. In pet Spaniels, it is satisfactory to use clippers or thinners to remove this hair and do natural feet, although a domed shape is what is preferred in the show type.

Clipped Cocker Spaniels

Step 1 – Clip from behind the skull to the base of the tail with a #7F or #5F blade. Continue down the shoulder to the elbow and clip the hair on the side of the dog, slightly across the way rather than up and down. This should be continued to where the ribcage starts to turn in.

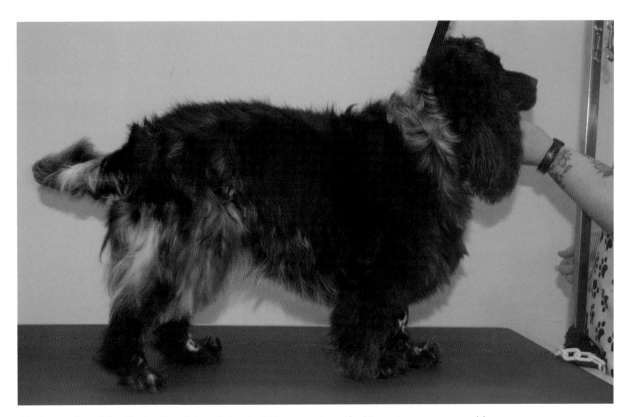

A hairy version of the Cocker Spaniel ready to start his groom to make his coat more manageable.

Step 2 – Clip down the back leg as shown in the image for Step 1 to just above the hock.

Step 3 – Clip from the chin to the top of the breastbone.

Step 4 – Remove all the hair from under the ears.

Step 5 – Thin the hair on the fronts and sides of the legs.

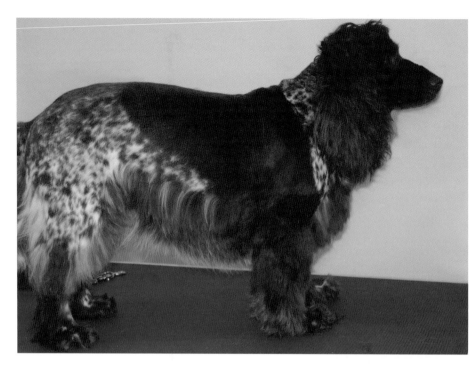

It is easy to see the clipping lines required for an easy method of hair removal instead of hand stripping.

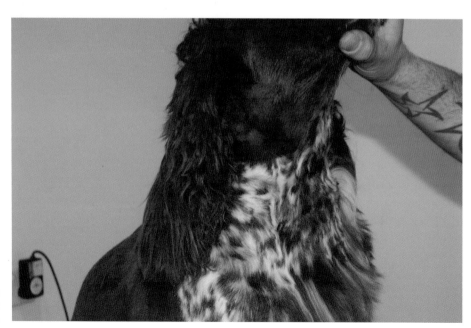

All excess hair under the throat makes the dog look stuffy in outline.

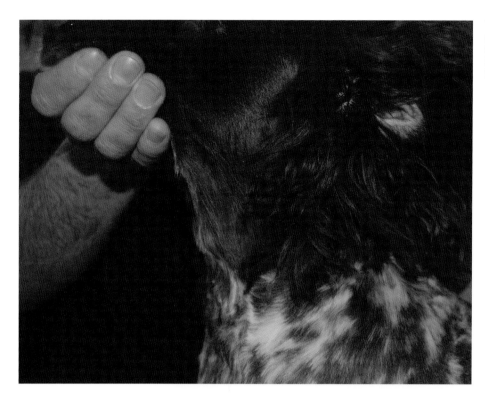

This hair is often matted due to people rubbing it when petting the dog. Removal of it is also healthier for the ears.

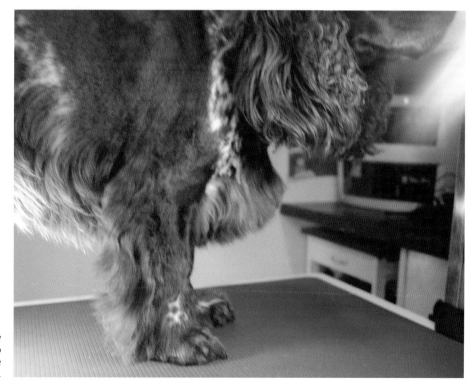

Much easier to keep tidy and groomed, with no excess showing on the outside.

Step 6 – Tidy all around the bottom of the back leg and tidy the feathering between the back legs in an A-shape.

Step 7 – Clip the top of the head to remove excess hair or leave the topknot if desired. Then thin off any longer hair to give a clean head and face.

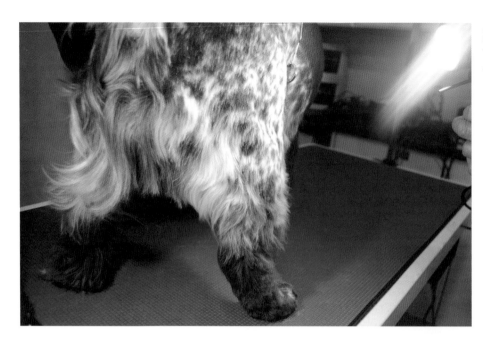

A before-and-after image showing how natural and tidy the hair can be with just a little trimming.

A traditional trim showing topknot removed and a clean head to enhance the Spaniel shape.

Step 8 – Remove any excess hair on the end of the tail and hold the tail straight out from the body having combed it thoroughly. Now trim from the tip to the base in a curve on either side.

Step 9 – Blend all of the clipped areas into the longer hair using thinning scissors parallel to the coat growth to remove evidence of where the clipping stopped.

Step 10 – Trim the feet in a natural shape as in the 'Natural Feet' section in Chapter 7.

Step 11 – Thin down or clip the top of the ear for about 2in (5cm) and blend the join between clipped and long hair with thinners.

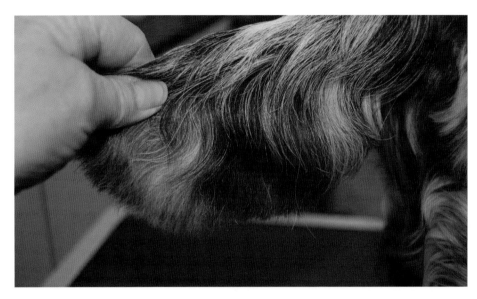

It is important not to raise the tail as you trim, otherwise the shape will be too long near the base.

A natural-shaped foot on a working-type Cocker. Show types would have their feet built up at the front.

The final procedure to achieving a well-groomed dog on the top of the ears. There is not as much removed as in a show Cocker.

Trimming a Setter

All of the Setters have the body stripped in the same fashion. However, there are some slight differences in the ear style and technique between them. The use of a banded comb is an excellent way to remove the body hair.

We can begin with the Irish Setter as a template for styling the others. The throat and sides of neck need to be thinned in the UK. In the US, the trimming is done using clippers much more than we do. Clipping causes a colour change here.

Step 1 – Starting at the hairiest area under the lips, thin the longer hair or tufts that, when viewed from the side, spoil a clean outline. This can be taken really short and smooth. You need to hold the dog's head completely upwards to avoid catching any of the loose skin on the throat.

Step 2 – Remove all of the hair that grows downwards to the breastbone using your thinning scissors and you will notice there is a join at each side where the hair starts to grow in a different direction. You will also see that there is a little indentation at each side of the breastbone. Thin a little into this. You can blend the neck hair into the throat using your comb and thinners along the join.

Step 3 – Using thinners again, remove all of the excess hair from under the ears with thinning scissors so that they lie flat against the neck.

For Irish Setters – Using your finger and thumb or a stripping stone, begin to strip the top of the ears and down towards the tip to stop them looking bushy and

The orange belton colour of this English Setter is a favourite. They are known as 'a gentleman by nature'.

The beautiful, rich red coat of the Irish Setter. The most well-known of the Setter breeds.

A gorgeous black and tan coloured Gordon Setter. The largest of the Setter breeds.

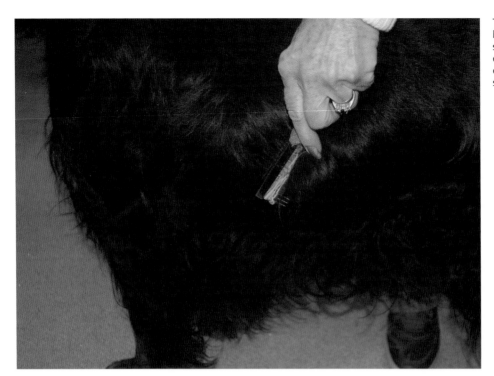

The use of the banded comb is shown here. This demonstrates how easy it is to use on silky coats.

A trimmed neck on Irish Setter showing how clean it should be when finished. This makes the neck more elegant.

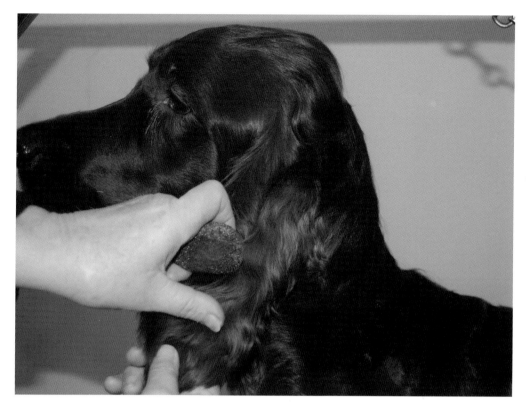

If you want avoid colour change in an Irish Setter, hand stripping is essential.

An English Setter ear before clipping showing the amount of hair to be clipped to achieve the correct ear style.

Long hair can be removed by clipping the ear of the English Setter according to the traditional grooming style of the country of origin.

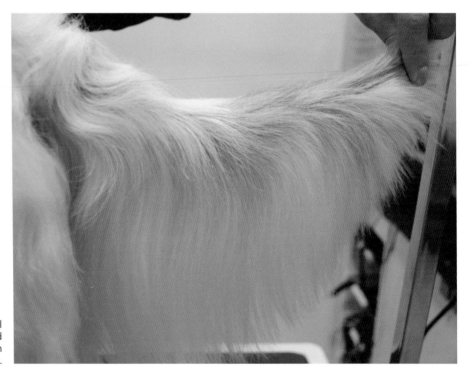

An example of a beautiful scimitar or sword-shaped tail shown on this English Setter.

unruly. Leave the fringe at the front of the ear that folds back as this gives a lovely soft expression. Once enough hair is off the outside of the ears you can trim carefully from the base to the tip and then from the bottom of the fringe to the tip on the opposite side.

For English Setters – Using a #10 blade on a trimmer, remove the hair from the base of the ear to the tip, leaving the same fold at the front, and scissor round the edge as above. Blend the join between the top of the ear and the head with thinning scissors.

For Gordon Setters – Thin down the top of the ear to where the fold at the front ends, leaving the bottom of the ear covered with long hair.

Step 4 – All of the Setters have a natural foot shape; the hair can be removed from the hock to the heel with thinning scissors in the Irish and English Setter but not the Gordon, where the hair is only tidied and left padded.

Step 5 – Trim under the base of the tail with thinning scissors for about 1in (2.5cm). Do not take any off the top of the tail. This separates the tail from the body and also helps to keep the hair clean around the anus.

Step 6 – Holding the end of the tail and leaving a little to cover the tip, twist the hair round and then remove the excess from the end using your thinning scissors. A Setter's tail should ideally not go below the hock. Take hold of the tail and comb out thoroughly from the skin while holding it in line with the back. The hair can then be tipped on the feathering in a sword shape from both sides. Make sure you do not lift the tail up as you go as the hair will become longer towards the base by doing this.

This basic trim is suitable for all the Setters, allowing for the differences of the ears.

Dachshunds

This breed is unique as it is available in three different coat types and sizes so the grooming of them corresponds to the classification of the coat. The wire-coated type is stripped using the Border Terrier technique on the body while the legs are not taken quite as short. For a pet, you can scissor the legs to whatever length is suitable for your lifestyle. The long-coated variety is stripped like the Spaniels and Setters but with long ears and the smooths following the de-shedding process.

CHAPTER **9**

Flowing Tresses

Full Coats

This type of coat, sometimes referred to as a drop coat, can take quite a lot of care if you want to keep it long and in a glorious flowing condition. It is very interesting that when people go to their first few visits to a groomer after buying a pup of this type, they never want it to be cut, as they want to keep it looking glamorous. The sight of these lovely dogs gliding along is usually what attracted them to the breed in the first place so, in their mind, they see their puppy looking like this. What owners do not realize is that an enormous amount of work goes into keeping a full, natural coat like this. After a little while, they find that either the hair is too long for them to keep well because it gets full of burrs, the hair gets very dirty in wet weather, or the commitment taken to regularly groom them is taking up too much of their time.

This is when owners usually decide that they would prefer to have the dog cut shorter and also in a more manageable style. More often than not, the chances are that the dog has now become really matted at the skin because they think they are doing a good job brushing the dog when, in fact, they are only brushing the top layers of hair and leaving the undercoat untouched. When this happens, all the cast dead coat, being soft, tangles together as it accumulates at the roots, and eventually becomes a mat. Often these mats are so bad they result in the whole coat needing to be shaved off, to the annoyance of the owner and disappointment for the groomer who wants to be able to turn out a beautiful-looking dog.

For a show dog, it is important that there is still some undercoat but that it is not too excessive. A pet can have a little less, depending on the quality of its coat. Breeds of this type are Lhasa Apsos, Bearded Collies, Shih Tzus, Yorkshire Terriers, Maltese Terriers and so on. All of these breeds have a coat that falls down to the ground with a parting in the middle and is relatively straight. The best way to thoroughly groom these breeds is by using a soft slicker to begin with – not on a show coat, however, where a pin brush would be more appropriate. You can make grooming easier by starting at the undercarriage and lifting the hair up, keeping it out of the way by using a hair clip to fasten the hair up. I work in layers from there while using a spray, with either diluted conditioner or de-matting spray, and also using a hairdryer to separate the individual hairs as I work.

If you have any coat that you are trying to keep long, it is important that you do not comb or brush the dry hair as it will cause it to break off. Wet hair is more elastic and stretches when you brush it compared to dry hair, so remember to keep spraying the coat slightly. Continue, layer by layer, so that you are brushing each layer into a knot-free under layer. Work your way right up the side of the dog until you reach the spine. Repeat this process from between the front legs all the way up to the chin. When you have brushed through all of the coat, repeat using a wide-toothed comb to make sure there are no stubborn tangles left in the entire coat, especially under the armpits.

When grooming the dog, the most important parts to be careful with, and to ensure they are groomed out

OPPOSITE: This is a super example of a natural coat; however, it requires constant attention to look good.

115

This is a good method to use to be able to see underneath the dog as you groom. You could use the clips if you are clipping off the undercarriage too.

thoroughly, are under the armpits, between the back legs, the heels and under the ears. These areas are always ones that are missed and soon become a real problem to groom out. Also, always check that the comb is going right to the skin on the ends of the ears as this is often where it tends to glide over the top of the hair and the ends become felted. Unfortunately, when this happens, it is not kind to try to de-mat with a mat breaker or brush as often the ears will start to bleed from the constant tugging of the fine skin in this area.

Another problem with this area getting matted is that the dog can develop a haematoma, which is a blood-filled, cushion-like blood blister. This can occur if the ear has been very matted and needs to be shaved off. The mats actually begin to compress the ear flap and restrict the blood flow to the ends so that, when the mat is released by clipping it off, the blood rushes to the bottom of the ear and sometimes starts to drip off the end. On many occasions, the blood pools at the bottom and fills up, forming what looks like a squashy cushion. This is, in fact, the skin that is filled up with blood.

If this happens when you are grooming there is no need to panic. You can use an ear protector hood to fold the ears over each other on top of the head but make sure you have some protection in the areas where the skin is in contact with another piece of skin. Use cotton wool or a dressing so that the ears do not rub on each other by placing some padding between the skin surfaces. Raising the ears in this manner means that gravity forces the blood supply in the opposite direction, therefore stopping the formation of any more problems and counteracting the flow of blood. Leave the ear protector on for a few hours but, obviously, do not leave the dog unsupervised. If the ears seem to have improved after that then there is nothing else you need to do.

Unfortunately, sometimes dogs start to shake their heads and cause the ears to bleed again as they find the sensation a little strange. If this happens, you will need to put the protector back on for a while. If the cushion-like bulge does not disappear or the dog will not stop shaking its head, it may be necessary to go to the vet for treatment to release the blood from the pouch. Sometimes you can tell if a dog has had a haematoma as you can feel the cartilage has become distorted and warped.

The solution here is not to let your dog get matted ears. I always advise groomers to have the owner wait when they are going to shave off ears like this so that they can see that the dog has not been cut. As an owner/novice groomer, you should be aware that this can happen before clipping matted ears so you know it is a possibility. As an owner, therefore, it is important that you know that this is something that is possible if you are home grooming and have allowed the dog's ears to become really thick with mats.

It is also a good idea to trim the anal area of these breeds so that no faeces gets stuck on the coat when they are defecating. If it sticks, it will gradually build up until the poor dog will be unable to pass a stool because the previous faeces have solidified and blocked the anal opening. If this is left, the dog will develop sore, weeping infections of the skin around the anus, which possibly become infested by maggots. Just trim the long hair carefully on either side of the anus, clearing a little above and underneath the opening as well so that there is free passage for the faeces to come out cleanly. Do not trim down as far as the vulva or testicles.

Having given the dog a thorough brush and comb through, you can bath the dog now. If you have a dog with a problem coat, such as brittle or sparse hair, it is a good idea to use hot oil or a treatment on the ends of the hair prior to bathing. This will help bond the ends of the hair together and keep them strong. The treatment can be warmed in hot water and then applied to the dry or wet coat, according to the instructions, while the dog is in the bath, using it before shampooing. Always check the directions on the label to ensure the optimum success when using the product as they may vary. Make sure you leave the treatment on the coat for the correct length of time, as too short an application can result in it having no effect, while too long a treatment may make it greasy. Once this has been applied, you can begin to apply your chosen shampoo. There is a huge choice of shampoos available, and each one claims to be the ultimate one, to solve all problems. In general, a conditioning one would be best. These types of coat need lots of moisture and continual looking after if in full coat.

The diluted shampoo should be gently squeezed through the coat, rather than rubbed, to ensure you don't break any of the hair. I usually apply the shampoo and rinse twice, once to clean and once to nourish. It is also very important that you wash the faces of these dogs thoroughly to remove any eye discharges or food build-up in the lips that have accumulated. It is sometimes preferable to use a shampoo specially designed for faces as it will not sting the eyes and may be formulated to deal with food or saliva staining, but it is not essential, as care should be

taken around these areas anyway. The underneath and the inside of the ear flap tends to get quite greasy too so this is another area that needs good and thorough washing to remove stubborn dirt from the ears.

When the coat has been thoroughly rinsed, with no sliminess remaining on any area of the coat, you can apply a conditioning rinse. Again, there are many products out there in pet stores and grooming supply shops, so it is probably trial and error as to which one you prefer. Not all products work the same on every dog so you can have a little fun trying out a few. The only thing I would say is, do not think cheap is a good option as, sometimes, if you look at the dilution rate on each, a more expensive product may be more economical in the end.

With this type of coat I would not necessarily blast them but would be more inclined to squeeze the coat after bathing with some towels, or drying cloths that are similar to a chamois leather and are readily available. This again prevents any tangling of the long hair. Remove as much of the water as you can before lifting the dog from the bath and check that you cannot squeeze any excess water from the ears, feet or tail prior to removing from the bath. This avoids overlong use of the dryer or water being dripped across the floor to the grooming table. When you have got your dog on the table again, begin by using a pin brush and dry from under the body in a methodical way. This will ensure the whole of the dog is completely dry by grooming layer by layer. You can again pin up the extra hair with a clip when doing this.

Try not to use a slicker on any of the finer coats if possible, unless you still need to remove some stubborn tangles. Check that under the dog's ears and the sides of the face and head do not have any damp patches by the time you finish drying. It is also important that you try to dry the coat in the direction of growth so that it lies flat to the body and is not blown upwards, as this will tangle the coat and cause ruffs along the back and sides, thereby spoiling the sleek appearance. It is also preferable to use a cooler setting on the dryer to avoid overheating the coat and drying out the oils. When everything is clean and dry, and the coat is knot free, you can begin to trim the dog up into a shape and style.

It is always a good idea to have the dog's nails cut prior to doing the feet as it can make it difficult to scissor efficiently around the edges if the nails are long (*see* Chapter 3). As we are considering pet trims only in this book, we can do a little judicial trimming to keep the dog clean and easier to manage, even if we are keeping the hair long. Using your small foot scissors, trim under the pads of the foot and make sure you remove any knots from this area with the tips of your scissors. Also, check for knots between the toes, as this can be quite sore for the dog if left. There are often badly matted areas under the pads, which can make walking difficult and painful for the dog if they are left. Comb the hair down over the foot and trim neatly across the front of it. Now, comb the hair to the sides and trim around the foot in a circular shape to round it off. Comb the hair in every direction and ensure that no matter when you do so, it should still be rounded. Try not to cut up the leg at all, just around where the foot touches the floor.

If you decide to have a full coat at this point, it is up to you what length you want the skirt to be. It can be full length, medium length or quite a bit shorter. This can be done by using longer scissors, beginning at the groin area; hold up the penis on males and begin to cut in a slightly sloping line from there to right between the front legs, so that the bottom of the chest hair is the longest part of the skirt. If your dog gets very muddy underneath the body, it is possible to remove the belly hair completely, using a #7F blade, and leave a fringe on either side of the body so that the dog still looks like a full coat but, in fact, only has side hair. The clipped panel is free from hair and helps to keep that area free from dirt and knots if the coat gets wet often, especially in the winter.

Using a Comb Attachment for a Puppy Trim

An alternative way to trim these coats is with the use of a comb attachment and blade (*see* Chapter 2). I would not use this method on a Yorkshire Terrier though as the coat is rather fine for this type of grooming. You can choose whichever length you fancy by trying out the combs on the coat, but remember to start with one you think is going to be longer than required. It is imperative that the coat is well prepared before using a comb attachment as it will snag if there are any knots and can result in a gouge being made in the coat. This will look very unsightly and can be difficult to correct.

Step 1 – Start at the back of the head and clip to the base of the tail. Continue down the sides and throat area of the dog. You can decide if you want the dog to have a skirt or not at this point. If not, continue underneath the body as well. Bring the clipper down the tops of the front legs only and down three quarters of the back leg. Also bring your clipper down the very back of the leg to where the

Try to avoid cutting from the side to the front as it results in a point at the front of the foot instead of a round shape.

If hair around the foot is left too long, it trails on the ground and gets very dirty.

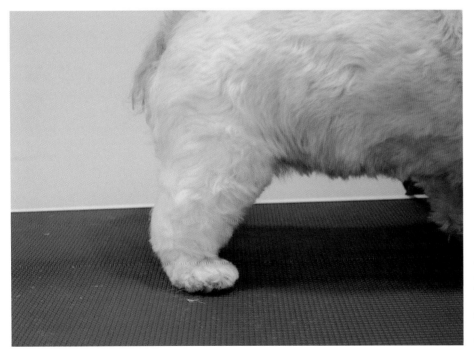

The curvy shape of the rear gives more interest to the hindquarters. Unfortunately, this little dog is lacking hair at the bottom of the legs due to an allergy.

119

bend is. Check this by lifting the leg up and bending the leg. If you look at the diagram you will see where this needs to end.

Step 2 – Using your thinners or scissors, carefully cut down from the hock to the heel area on the back leg; then continue around the sides by lifting the hair upwards with a comb and scissoring downwards to make the leg look padded.

Step 3 – Stand at the front of each back leg and scissor the longer hair in a curve, to neaten the shape, following the natural angles of the leg.

Step 4 – Stand behind the dog then tidy up the inside of the legs to make them neat and in balance with the rest of the groom.

Step 5 – With the dog now facing to the front, lift the leg hair on the front leg upwards and outwards using the comb, so that it stands out from the leg.

Step 6 – Now, using your thinners or scissors, cut downwards to make a straight line on the outside and inside of the front leg to neaten it and ensure that the leg is not sloping inwards with the top too wide at the elbows. When standing at the side of the dog, trim the front of the leg line straight down to the toes. Never aim towards the pastern.

Step 7 – Standing behind the dog, scissor the excess hair from the back of the front legs, making the shape slightly longer at the top than the bottom, and bring the scissors neatly in at the heel with no untidy hair left here.

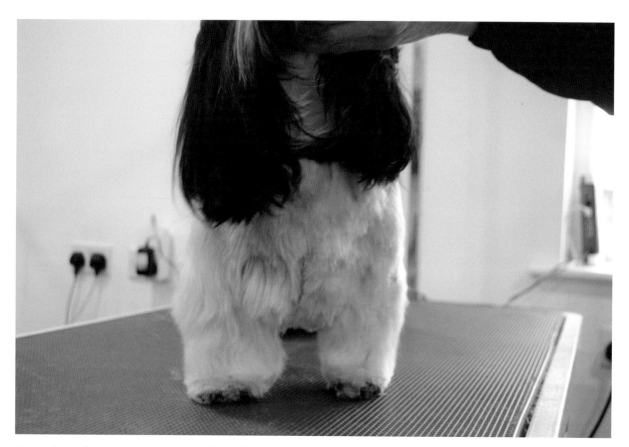

Comparison of trimmed and untrimmed leg with no hair sticking out at the elbows.

Step 8 – When grooming and trimming the tail, the length can be adjusted to whatever shape you want. Begin by combing down all the hair so that there are no curly bits on the top. Hold the tail outwards in line with the back and scissor, using long scissors, from the tip to the base in a curved shape. Try to avoid lifting the tail upwards as you go along the line. Then repeat the procedure on the other side. You can also trim a V-shape at the top of the tail to neaten the appearance a little. This just allows the top of the tail to flow into the rest of it without any unsightly bulges, giving it a more professional style.

If you want a shorter trim on the body, you can use a blade to remove excess hair instead of a blade and comb attachment. This will enable you to have the body much shorter and more manageable. This is also a good way to make your dog look slimmer. You can use a #4F, 5F# or #7F blade on its own, depending on what length you think is suitable for your preference and for the finish on the dog's coat.

Starting at the back of the skull, again clip to the base of the tail, following the hair growth, and remove the excess hair from the body. Do this slowly so that you avoid clipping any warts or growths as you go along. Only clip in the direction of the growth and not against it as, if you do so, you will cut the hair much shorter in those areas where the direction is reversed. You can leave the legs full and then blend them into the body with thinning scissors when you have finished the clipper work. Remember to clip under the body as well if you are having no skirt. The shaping can then be done in the same way as before. Make sure all joins are neat and not sticking out, by looking from the front to check that your leg is straight when you see it from all directions. When trimming the front of the leg, make sure you always cut to the toes and do not be tempted to cut into the pastern, as this makes the

More hair is needed at the front of this foreleg to stop the curved appearance.

One of the head styles you can try if you have a full-coated dog. Sometimes even the clipped ones can look attractive in this style too.

Bunches on this dog show off his lovely expression and coat condition.

shape of the leg look like a banana with the foot sticking out from the leg.

Stand at the back of the front leg and gently trim from the elbow into the heel with long scissors. The longest hair should be at the top. When trimming the front of the back legs, face the front of the leg and scissor round in a curve to the bottom, making sure that you have combed all of the hair from the inside of the leg area. Follow on by trimming between the back legs. Try to remember to make your legs balanced with the rest of the groom and not out of proportion. Put your dog onto the floor and let him have a shake to settle all the hair, and have a good look to see if there are any areas that still need to be tidied.

When grooming the head of these breeds, there are many possibilities for style and shape that can be varied. You may like to have the topknot long and tied up with a latex or wool band, or a shorter, sassy version. If doing a longer topknot, comb the hair on the top of the head back and then make a parting across the head just behind the eyes. Take this hair and put in your band, twisting it three or four times depending on the elasticity of the type you choose. You can add a bow over this if you want then,

taking your scissors, trim off the untidy ends of hair by combing the bunch upwards and scissoring across the hair.

You can, if you wish, make a parting in the hair from ear to ear and, using your comb, part from the outside corner of the eye; then part a line from between the eyes to the back of the middle parting to join this up, and put in your bands at the top of the ear. Now repeat by doing the same on the other side. You can again put in a pair of matching bows just above the ears if you want. This is particularly nice on Maltese and Lhasa Apsos. As another alternative, you could add plaits to the styling of the head and gather them behind the head with a band or bow.

If you decide to do a shorter trim, you can still keep the topknot but shorten the chin and cheeks: comb all the hair downwards while holding the dog's head up so that you get all the hair combed through thoroughly, then scissor across and under the chin in a straight line. Comb the hair down from the side of the face then, starting at the front, scissor in a curve to under the ear. Repeat as before on the other side. Be very careful you don't cut across the hair on the cheek, always underneath the jaw

All ready to go to a special occasion with his fancy plaits.

A little more hair could be removed from the chin and nose to enhance a rounder head.

line. You can keep the ears long and combed down, by scissoring round them in a curve, or blended into the same length as the head. Follow the line you have done previously for the side of the face after checking where the ear leather ends, and then trim around to the same length.

If you do not want a topknot, you can shorten the top of the head by using your comb and thinning scissors, a comb attachment against the growth or even a blade. With the dog facing towards you, lift up the hair at the back of the head with your comb so that it stands up off the head. Remove as much hair as you want off with your thinning scissors, using the comb as a guide. Always have your comb positioned across the head and not up and down the way. Once you have cut the first row of hair at the back of the head, put your comb in again to include the next layer and some of the previously cut

coat. This will give you a guide as to the length of every subsequent cut.

Continue forwards with each cut until you get to the eyebrows. After combing all the hair on the top of the head through to check that it is even, comb the eyebrow hair forwards and trim a visor across the eyes from outside one eye to the outside of the other, ensuring you are not tempted to cut up onto the head hair. Finally, just use your thinning scissors to tidy up the lines.

Quite an attractive head shape can be made by clipping off the ears with a #10 blade, with the growth, outside and in and then by carefully scissoring around the ear from the base to the tip; then hold the ear upwards and pull down the hair on the edges of the ear so that the hair stands proud of the ear. Put your nail at the edge of the ear so that you will not cut the ear and, going from the base, carefully use your nail to protect the ear edge from the scissor. Use small scissors for this so that you are aware of where the whole of the blade is at all times. Turn the ear around and carefully repeat on the other side. You can proceed as before with the rounding of the chin and sides of the face; however, this time, you are going to start to use your chunkers or thinners around the head and face to shorten the whole shape into a ball. Do this by carefully taking off a small amount of hair at a time and remember to include the muzzle and chin. Dogs can look really cute like this and it also helps prevent ears becoming matted.

Another variation of this style is to give them a Terrier head for variety. For this you need to clip the top of the head and cheeks with a #5F or #7F blade, leaving everything in front of an imaginary line between the outside corner of the eye to the corner of the lip. You can give the dog a visor as before, or split the eyebrows into two by removing the hair from between them with thinning scissors. Comb all the hair, then you can decide what style you want to do the foreface –round or beard?

This trim can look nice if the rest of the dog is in a shorter trim and not in a full coat.

Yorkshire Terriers

Yorkshire Terriers have such lovely coats but do tend to get very matted if they are not regularly groomed. It is not just the body that gets matted but especially the legs, as this is where I find owners are not usually particular enough. I think this is due to the fact they are afraid of injuring their little pet. It is possible to keep them in full coat but, if you choose this style, you may want to shorten the skirt a little to make it tidier using the same method used in the 'Using a Comb Attachment for a Puppy Trim' section. Under the pads can be scissored carefully to remove any knots and excess hair. Make sure the Yorkshire Terrier has its nails cut regularly as they can become really overgrown and cause foot problems, as well as potentially growing into the feet. Do not forget dew claws as these may be situated on the hind legs as well as the front. You can scissor round the foot to tidy. Under the tail, the anal area will need to be cleaned too to keep it free from soiling.

If you are tying up the topknot in the Yorkshire Terrier, you can also clip the tips of the ears with a #10 blade outside and in for about a third of the top of the ear, and trim the edge of the area you have just clipped. Do not go to the base of the ears when scissoring. I find that if you want to have your Yorkshire Terrier in a shorter trim, it is better to do this with the scissors and comb in the same way as the top of the drop-coat head. This can take a little practice to begin with. Just remember not to go too short in the beginning as it will be difficult to correct with such little coat.

The most popular trim we have for a Yorkshire Terrier is where the body is clipped with a #7F from the Adam's apple, which is the lump in the throat area of the dog, to the top of the breastbone. This is the bone that sticks out on the front of the chest. Clip from under the ear to the elbow and down the sides of the dog, to just above the bottom of where the body ends. Leave this long hair on here to make the skirt. Clip down the outside of the back leg to clear away excess hair. Tidy all the areas you have clipped that join into longer hair by using the thinning scissors so that no ridge remains. Shape in between the back legs by doing an A-shape and by angling the scissors from the vulva or testicles to the hock. The skirt needs to be blended along the sides by pointing your thinning scissors downwards, not across the coat, and using them in a running fashion – that is, not keeping them in one place and cutting, but moving them along continuously as you cut to make a well-blended line with no holes and missed spots.

The skirt line can be cut but, again, make sure you lift up the penis on a male so that you do not cut it by mistake. Shape the skirt by sloping slightly from the groin direction to between the front legs, which is the longest part of the skirt. You can finish off with a little coat gloss or anti-static spray, as these coats can have a lot of static to work with. Using anti-static sprays also means they can be groomed out much more easily without it flying away. I would like to mention here about de-matting sprays. These do not remove great big mats of hair once they are formed, but are more to flatten down the hair shafts that have become intertwined and tangled together. These should be used for minor tangles or as a preventative measure while doing routing grooming.

CHAPTER 10

The Fluffies

Wool Coats

There are quite a few breeds that have what is considered to be a wool coat. Poodles, Bichons and most of the cross breeds that have a poodle in their make-up are some of them. These coats can be awkward to keep because as soon as they get wet they will felt into solid clumps if left to dry naturally and not brushed dry every time. Styling of these types of coat is really important so that the shape you choose is suitable for your lifestyle. Lots of people want a fluffy dog; however, the time involved to have this style may not be achievable. The simplest way for a novice groomer to keep their dog in shape is to clip it off short. The head and tail can be trimmed to give it a little style. This is the less technical of trims but still can need a bit of practice to do safely.

The first mistake most pet owners make after deciding to try to groom their own dog is that they do not always buy suitable tools for the type of coat. Slicker brushes that have bobbles on the end of each pin to prevent the dog from getting scratched are not suitable for wool coats. I have found that this type of slicker, if used on a long or wool coat, often gets the hair tangled around the bobbles, causing discomfort to the dog as it makes the hair snag more. Slicker brushes with bent pins of various firmness are best when dealing with most coats and they are especially important with wool types of coat. This is because they fluff the hair up in a desirable fashion and make it stand out from the body or legs so that it is suitable for final scissoring. Bristle brushes, or the twin-sided type of brushes with straight pins on one side and bristles on the other, are again unsuitable for this coat. A good-quality comb with wide and narrower teeth is a great investment as you can take out the tangled hair more gently by using the wide end first before the narrower end to check that it is knot free.

It is usually a good idea to use a quality conditioner on these coats after bathing to reduce static and make the coat easier to comb through. This will also flatten the hair shaft and make it smooth so that there is less likelihood of the coat becoming matted for a while. I find that blasting is a great time saver and straightener in these situations and should be done thoroughly if the dog is tolerant of the process. I always use an ear protection hood for these dogs as they can be quite sensitive to the noise. When these coats are being brushed, they should be done with short, light, quick strokes, making sure the hair is stretched from the roots. This is known as 'fluff drying'. Fluff drying has to be done well to achieve a good finish on the dog's coat. Never leave any of these coats partially dried as they will mat very easily if not groomed thoroughly to the skin. The success of grooming wool-coated breeds is in the preparation.

The Poodle

This is an easy trim and can be used for Poodles and Poodle crosses.

OPPOSITE: Some dogs love having a little cuddle when being groomed. Who could resist him?

This old gentleman is in an easy-to-keep style for a novice. He is just chilling, waiting for his bath.

Step 1 – Having thoroughly prepared the dog so that there are no knots in the coat, use a clipper with a #10, #15 or #30 blade and choose a comb attachment that gives you the length you like. You can clip them over all of the coat and legs to give an even finish. You may want to use a longer attachment on the legs to give a little more style. Make sure you continue under the chest and ribcage when clipping the body.

Step 2 – Using your long, straight scissors, remove any stray ends that appear when you lift the coat away from the leg until all of the coat is even and tidy.

Clean Feet on a Poodle

When doing the feet, you may want them to be clean with no hair or just the same length as the legs. In either case, with a wool coat it is advisable to clip out the undersides of the feet between the pads with a #30 blade. This prevents matting of the wool coat, especially when they get wet.

Step 1 – Lift the front foot up and, using a trimmer on a #30 blade setting, clip under the foot and remove all the hair.

Step 2 – The next step, if doing a traditional trim, is to bring the foot forwards and hold it towards you. Use your clipper to remove the hair against the growth to the top of the toes only. Do not go up as far as the ankle as it spoils the look of the legs. Press your middle finger under the pads (this spreads the toes apart) and carefully remove the hair from the edges of the nails and between the toes. Take care to ensure that you go above the webbing between the toes when you are removing the hair from this area and not straight up between the toes, as you will cut the loose skin here if you do it in the latter manner.

Round Feet on a Poodle or Doodle

Step 1 – Remove the hair from under the pads as before and ensure there are no knots between the toes.

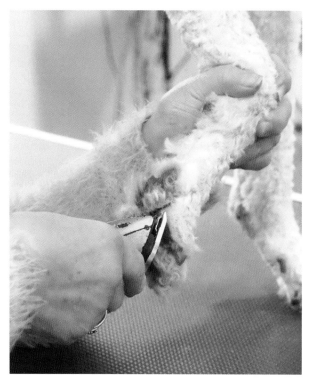

There should be no hair at all left after clipping the foot. Do not be tempted to use a longer blade as it will be much more difficult to get a good finish.

Never clip right up to the ankle in a Poodle as it spoils the overall appearance and is very dated.

Step 2 – With the foot on the ground, trim the foot in a circular shape to remove any hairs around the toes that are on the ground.

Clean Face on a Poodle
Clip against the growth carefully from the Adam's apple to the very end of the lips, removing any hairs from the chin. Using the edge of the clipper blade, make a straight line from the outside edge of the eye to the front of the ear, removing all of the hair in front of it. When this is completed, join up the clipped areas to form the line that would be in place if a necklace was worn. Now remove the hair from the bridge of the nose by clipping the hair against the growth from a line level with the eyes. Be careful not to go too high up between the eyes as it is essential that this is left to form part of the topknot.

Now that you have the basic lines drawn for the shape of the clipped area of the face, remove the hair from under the eye by pulling the lower eyelid down while you carefully clip upwards so that you do not end up with a panda look. Only do this if you are confident you can do it safely. Finally, remove all of the hair inside this imaginary necklace line against the growth to get a clean, even finish. When clipping the lip area, make sure you pull the lip back to get a flat surface. The hair should be clipped against the growth on the face

Moustache
If you decide to do this style, the moustache should be well forward on the nose and not behind the edge of the lip. Clip the rest of the face as before until under the jaw, in line with edge of the mouth. Comb the hair forwards and remove any untidy hair on the front of the face. Proceed to trim with scissors or chunkers to make the moustache round like a doughnut. This style is useful if you have a dog with an undershot or overshot bite as it draws the attention away from the mouth area. It is also

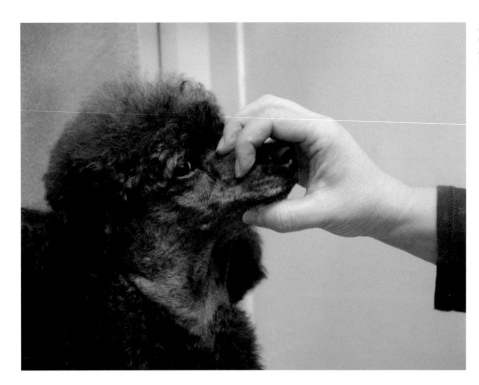

A clipped face keeps the eyes and mouth clean and this is the traditional Poodle style.

attractive on very masculine dogs or useful on those who are sensitive to being clipped on the front of the face.

Clean Tail

Using your #30 blade or longer, whichever length you prefer, remove all of the hair from the tail including the underside. This gives a more masculine style and, combined with shaved ears, makes a more distinct style for a male. Clip the ears with a #10, #15 or # 30 blade on the trimmers and finish by scissoring around the ears. Hold the ear upwards and pull the hair on the edge away from the ears, then scissor carefully from the base to the tip. This is a very healthy trim and keeps the ears free from hair that prevents air getting into the ear to keep it clean. This is a very smart stallion-like trim.

Topknot on a Poodle

The topknot can be quite tricky to do well. Begin by combing all of the hair upwards and outwards, and scissor off the excess at the sides of the face and back of the skull, being careful not to cut into the head. When doing the front of the head, try to cut straight up or slightly

curved, whichever you prefer, but never sloping into the top of the head. When you have done this and have no unsightly bits hanging down, start to curve over the top of the head to form a cap. Look at the head from all angles; it should be symmetrical and tidy when viewed from every direction.

Tidying Up and Finishing

Tidy any stray ends on the body area with long or short, straight scissors, depending on the length of the area you are cutting. If you were trimming the legs of a dog, for example, you would use your longer scissors so that you get an even cut on the whole length of the blade rather than little irregular snips.

The Traditional Poodle Tail

Using your #30 blade on your trimmers, remove approximately 1–2in (2.5–5cm) of hair from the base of the tail against the growth, depending on the size of the poodle. Never shave any more than this, otherwise it ends up as a big stalk and a pom-pom at the very end. When styled like this, it is a dead giveaway that an amateur has trimmed the

No knots in these ears and they are very hygienic too.

This well-trimmed head tops off even the most basic of trims.

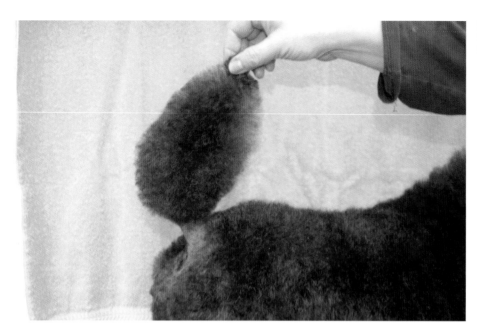

No long stalk and tiny pom-pom for a professional look.

dog. Be extremely careful when you are clipping around the anus to avoid damage. Hold the tail upwards to where it would sit when a dog is on the ground and moving. Next, make the end into a bunch and scissor the excess off the end of the tail, being careful to leave a small amount over the bone to protect it. While holding the tail up by the tip and in the correct position, shake the tail gently and comb it, allowing the hair to fan outwards. Now take your scissors and, using the tips, lift the hair from underneath and cut it in a circular fashion to the tip, making a ball or oval as you gradually work around the whole tail; keep combing it out all throughout the process.

More Stylish Trim

If you want a bit more shape to your trim, complete the feet, face and tail as before. This time you are going to clip the body but leave a bit of length on the legs. The body can be clipped with a comb attachment or blade to whatever length you prefer. The only criteria is that the legs should be slightly longer than the body and should never taper in at the bottoms. Once you have clipped the body, do not continue down the legs, but blend the join from body to legs with scissors or a comb attachment if that is what was used. Do not come in at the bottom of the legs when scissoring. Starting at the bottom of the cuff, comb

all the hair downwards and remove the excess hair that is falling over the feet. When this has been completed, begin with the front legs and bevel the bottom of the leg upwards into the longer hair length so that it curves up from the foot.

Position the dog towards you, use your long scissors and cut a line on the outside and inside of the leg to straighten the outline and remove any bumps. Do the same to areas at the bottom of the leg with excess hair that is spoiling the straight leg effect. When you have done this, stand at the side of the dog and look at the front line of the dog. The leg should never look like a banana when viewed from the side so make sure you look at the line from the shoulder to the bottom of the cuff. This should never be concave when standing from the side.

When you start to trim the back leg, scissor the front of the hind leg by standing to face towards the back leg; come straight down to the knee first and then sweep carefully from the knee into the foot a little more sharply. This helps to give the leg shape rather than being straight up and down. By trimming the back of the hind leg from the point of the buttock to the back of the knee area in as tightly as you can, you can then sweep out from the back of the leg to the hock and shape the foot to the hock so that it sits out and gives a shape to the leg.

Longer leg hair and a more bevelled finish to the bottom of the leg give a more attractive style.

Miami Trim

In this trim, most of the body and legs are removed except for an area at the bottom of the legs. When deciding where to put the bracelets, begin with the back legs. Find an area about 1in (2.5cm) above the hock and scissor a line sloping slightly downwards to the front. Match the height of those on the front leg but do not slope these ones; just scissor round evenly in a straight line. Comb the hair down and remove excess from the cuffs; then make a circle around the middle of the bracelet. Begin to curve the bottom half of this into the foot and the top half into the leg. This is an attractive trim on a bitch when the owner finds it difficult to keep all of the legs knot free, especially if she has a more active lifestyle.

Ear Shapes

There are quite a few different ear shapes that can be used on any of these Poodles or Poodle crosses. A bobbed style is popular and can be done by combing the hair on the ear down to begin with, then carefully trimming around the ends in a curved fashion. Once you have done this, lift the hair on the outside of the ear outwards towards you. Begin to scissor with curved scissors, thinners or chunkers outwards and upwards, across the grain of the hair and towards the base of the ear, to give a rounded shape. Carefully, keep combing the hair outwards and repeating the process until you have a really even finish. Trim around the bottom of the ear again to ensure there are no long ends underneath or at the edges of the ears.

Tassels can also be done on these breeds if you fancy them. You can either have them coming straight across the ear or in a diamond shape if you prefer. Start off by clipping down the ear from the base with a #10, #15 or #30 blade. Continue to about two-thirds of the way down the ear and ensure the line is clean. When you have done this, scissor the edges of the tassel outwards so that it flares out to the side. Then trim around the edges straight across.

Alternatively, you can trim them a little differently if you want. I actually prefer this way but it is up to you. Trim down the ear with the same blades but this time make an inverted V-shape, starting again with the point at the top about two-thirds of the way down the ear. Clip the top of the diamond shape on the ear leather and scissor the same shape on the hair hanging down below it so that it comes to a point there too.

You can also try shaving the ears of a Bichon or Poodle cross, as they look so sassy like this. Using a #10, #15, #30 or #40 blade, shave down the whole ear and then carefully, by trimming to the outside edges, remove all of the hair on the ear inside and out. Take great care when

This trim means there is virtually no maintenance required for a Poodle owner who finds it difficult to keep the knots at bay.

Such a cutie with her bobbed ears. Just make sure they match. You will not have any problem with them being in her food either.

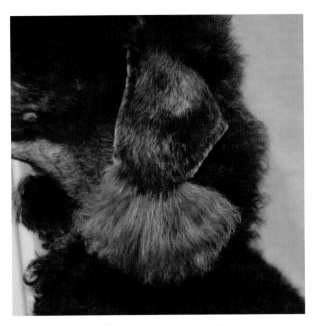

Something a little different if you are confident enough to try a new style.

trimming around the fold at the back of the ear not to catch the blade on the split area. Finish this style by scissoring carefully, with your nails at the edge of the ear flap and trimming from the base direction to the tip at all times.

In some of these breed styles, you may have opted for long ears, which can be a bit of a nuisance when feeding or watering the dog. If you want to prevent the ears becoming dirty or wet, you can band them so that the ear is less likely to go into the water or feed bowl. This can be done using the woolly bands available for human hair. These come in all sorts of colours and are available in large bags if required. Begin by combing the ears downwards and then wrapping the band around the ear two or three times, avoiding the ear leather at all times. Please take great care here and, as a precaution, take your comb and insert it between the ear leather and the band; this way there will be no part of the ear actually inside the band. If this happens it can have dire consequences, as the blood supply will be cut off and the ear will eventually fall off. The pain that the dog will suffer in the process is

No soggy ears here but proceed with caution when banding near the leathers.

What a stunning little Cavapoo paying a visit to the groomers.

severe so this step is so important if you band the ears. An alternative is to use a snood when feeding. This can make a huge difference to dogs who chew their ears when eating their food.

Doodles and Poodle Crosses

These are very popular nowadays. However, because the breeds are crossed with a wool coat, they can be quite a challenge to keep. I get really frustrated when I hear that some breeders have told owners that their dogs do not need to be groomed till they are over a year old. On the contrary, these dogs need constant care from an early age if they are not going to get badly matted. If you are going to go to a groomer, you need to have this type of dog on a regular schedule as well as working on them at home. This coat is not suitable for getting wet as, like all the wool or wool crosses, when left, it will mat very quickly

if not dried with a hairdryer while being groomed out thoroughly as soon as the dog comes home.

When it comes to styling these breeds, most people like the cuddly, fluffy and a little scruffy look. Begin by choosing what length of coat you would like on your dog and use your chosen comb attachment over a #10, #15 or #30 blade. Usually this will be a shorter body than the legs to give it a bit of style. Do a trial run on the rump as this is the most easily blended area if it is not to your liking. Starting at the occiput, behind the head, clip towards the base of the tail. Continue down the sides, following the way the coat is growing, although this type of coat is very forgiving. This is because the coat tends to grow in different directions, so there are usually no obvious clipper marks that can be seen as with other types of coat, due to the waviness or curliness of it.

Clip down from the Adam's apple to between the legs and onto the chest. Make sure you keep checking that your clipping is done neatly with no missed areas. You can then proceed down the top of the legs to blend in any long hair that prevents a straight leg from being shaped the same as the Poodle previously. On the back leg, try to carve a shape from under the buttock to sweep out towards the hock. Lift the leg and bend it to find the shortest part in line with the stifle, then sweep outwards, forming a curve.

You can do a teddy-shaped foot on these types of dogs if they have hairy legs, as some Doodles do not have long hair. Beginning at the front feet, trim under the pads as before. Then, beginning at a suitable height above the foot and on the leg hair, mark a line around the leg that will be the top of your styled foot. Scissor round the base of the foot and then layer it outwards towards the line around the leg. Trim the base of the foot that is in contact with the ground and start to curve the hair upwards and outwards for around 2–3in (5–7.5cm), depending on the size of the dog to arrive at your leg band. This will form a bevel. Repeat on the hind feet and make sure they are all at the same height. Following the shape of the leg, begin to scissor the remaining leg hair into the top of the bevel.

Tails on this type of dog are usually quite thick and sometimes top heavy at the base, so you can improve their shape by using your thinning scissors or chunkers to blend in the excess on the top and side of the tail. The remainder of the tail can be trimmed in a curve from the tip to the base, holding it straight out from tip to base and taking care not to lift it up as you trim.

The head is probably the most important part of these dogs' trim as it is the soft, soulful expression that attracts people to them in the first place. They often have very unruly curls that can prevent you getting a really even finish on them but, as long as you aim for the shape of the head as a whole, the dog will look attractive overall.

Step 1 – Having thoroughly combed all the hair through to ensure there are no knots in the cheeks or chin, begin by using your thinning scissors and carefully scissor the topknot into a curve that blends into the top of the ears. Try to ensure both sides are even.

Step 2 – Comb the head hair forwards towards the nose and trim a visor to frame the eyes. Try not to cut over the top of the head here and just go from the outside edge of one eye to the other. Remove the untidy hair between the eyes with thinners and again across the top of the

bridge and sides of the nose. Do not remove too much here, however – just enough to tidy the sides a little.

Step 3 – Hold the dog's chin and comb through the hair here to the root, then scissor across to make the underline tidy.

Step 4 – Comb down the side of the face and scissor underneath the cheek in a curve to join with the length of the ear. It is important that you keep combing this area while you are setting the line to avoid stray hair appearing at a later stage.

Step 5 – At the front of the face, comb the hair forwards in front of the nose and remove the untidy or discoloured sections.

Spanish Water Dogs

There are quite a few of this breed appearing now so I thought I would include them in this publication. Spanish Water Dogs have extremely tight curls that are really not suitable or meant for brushing out unlike other breeds. These dogs, as with most dogs with tight curls, benefit from swimming on a regular basis as this encourages the coat to keep the curl. The Curly Coated Retriever is also breed where regular swimming improves the coat.

The Spanish Water Dog is usually shaved off a few times a year and, after a bath, the coat again takes on its tightly curled appearance. For a pet owner, these breeds are extremely easy to keep as no regular brushing or combing is needed. They can also partake in rural walks and adventures without worrying about the coat being ruined and there are no worries if it is raining on a walk. For the Spanish Water Dog, a #7F blade is perfect for easily clipping the coat off all over. Within a few weeks they will have resumed their teddy-bear look and this will last for many months before needing to be clipped again. Ideally, you should gauge the time of clipping to accommodate the seasons and potential weather. These dogs definitely need to be started early as they are working dogs and can resent the process if not trained to accept the clippers early on. As with most of the Water Dogs, the coat is composed of curls to ensure the dog does not feel the cold after swimming in all weathers.

A neatly trimmed head on this Goldendoodle. The owner has followed the curve of the head and ears to achieve a super style and shape.

Bichon Frisé

Most Bichons that are kept as pets do not have the characteristic mane of hair left on their neck, as owners find it too difficult to keep groomed out. They can, however, still be groomed to retain the Bichon shape in general. As with Poodles and Poodle crosses, a comb attachment can be used for convenience; however this time, after clipping the body, do not go down the back leg but clip outwards from the hip. Remove the hair from the undercarriage too.

The front leg can be scissored as with the other wool-type coats in a straight line, and under the feet can be clipped out using a #30 blade on a trimmer and then scissored in a round shape. Stand behind the dog with it facing away from you and scissor a horseshoe shape around the profile of the rear. On the inside of the back leg, the shape is that of an A, close at the bottom of the inside of the foot. This shaping means that the outside of the rear foot is slightly longer than the inside. When scissoring the rear of the dog, form a curve ending just above the stifle and forming a peach-like bottom to join with the root of the tail. If you hold the tail over the body you will see any hair that is untidy at the root. Remove this to enhance the outline. No other trimming needs to be touched on the tail.

The head of the Bichon is an important feature of the breed. That cute, innocent-looking little dog with those expressive eyes would make anyone's heart melt. Around the eyes should be scissored clear of hair to show the desirable black rims, and the lips should be exposed too without making them look like they are lacking hair round about. A visor can be scissored from each outer edge of the eye with a slight peak in front. Starting at the top of the head and using curved scissors, carefully shape the hair in a circular fashion. On the sides of the face, the ears should be blended into the top of the head, keeping the roundness and with no separation of the ears. Working under the chin, scissor to ensure neatness and then scissor around the sides of the face from underneath while you are combing down and through the hair, blending in at the back of the head and into the ear shape.

It is extremely important when styling wool coats that the preparation is well done and the correct fluff-drying technique has been executed well. Straight preparation of the wool coat is less important in the Doodles whose coat tends to be much curlier than the Poodles, and the final style required is curly or wavy whereas the Poodle coat needs to be straight to be able to make an even finish when scissoring. If you fancy giving your wool-coated breeds a little bit of pizzazz, you can give them a fifties' wave look by spraying them after scissoring with a little water or water mixed with a little conditioner. Using a pin brush, lightly brush down the length of the hair and watch as your designer wave appears.

People always ask how a Poodle cross or indeed any cross should be groomed. The easy answer to this is to stand back and take a look at the dog. What breed does it look most like? Once you have decided this, just trim to the corresponding trim for that breed. Remember, unless you are showing your dog, you can style your dog in whatever way you fancy. Wool coats lend themselves to being able to have lots of different styles that can be changed from time to time. These are often the kind of dogs and coats that some people like to embellish with colour or hair ornaments.

There are quite a few different ways of colouring the dog by using chalks, sprays, mousses and wands, as well as the traditional wash-in dye. The main thing to remember is that you must use the proprietary products that are designed for use on dogs and not human products. These will be non-toxic and made to wash out very easily. This procedure is not something included within the scope of this book but, if this is something you would like to try, there are numerous books on the subject that provide lots of ideas for success in this field. You may just want to have a little sparkle for a special occasion or something more elaborate. The choice is yours to explore.

Interesting Fact

Poodle wool was used to make hats by felting the coat after it was removed and, after wetting the wool thoroughly, it was squeezed and rolled to make the felt material. You can also use the wool that you have clipped from your poodle to make into polishing cloths by just repeatedly squeezing it in your hands until you have formed a pad. This can then be used to polish wooden furniture.

Conclusion

I am so glad to have been given the opportunity to try to help owners understand a little about the processes involved in grooming their dog, and also some of the difficulties that can occur in doing this successfully. The great thing is that, even if you do not cut your dog, the condition of the coat and its manageability will be much improved just by understanding why and how things like mats occur when you think you have been doing a good job. I am sure that, with some practice, most of you will be able to keep your dog in a basic trim of which you can be proud. Just remember that grooming is a skill and, like all other skills, needs to be practised to gain confidence and the dexterity that will enable you to achieve a good standard of cut and style. The foundation of any groom is the preparation of the coat and, by trying to cut corners here, you will never get satisfactory results in your finish. I wish I had a pound for every time a student feels they are struggling to get knots out of the coat but, with some patience and practice they get there, resulting in a higher standard of work later on in the rest of the groom.

Having knowledge of types of equipment, how to use them and, importantly, how to look after them, means that you should not be struggling by using possibly ineffective tools for the wrong job. You need to have the basic tools to begin grooming but, gradually, you can add to these to give you more scope as you improve your skills. Good-quality grooming tools are not cheap but most should last you for years. You may need to replace blades, combs and so on but clippers, if regularly serviced, can last a very long time. I have clippers in my salon that are twenty-five years old and still going strong. When you groom your own dog, your family and friends will never need to wonder what to give you as a present, as a voucher for a good grooming supplier always goes down a treat.

If you have multiple dogs, your grooming bill will be substantially reduced. Although the style and finish may not be as good as a professional groomer, it will possibly be good enough for your requirements and may, indeed, spur you on to become a professional groomer too. I know that many people enjoy the training days for owners that we sometimes have and see their dog in a new light when it comes to being cooperative on a grooming table. They also realize how important it is not to have your dog running about on the table when you are trying to cut them. The grooming process offers a chance to have a good bond with your dog through touching and stroking, and as the dog ages, you can adjust the style of your groom according to the physical condition and health of the dog. It is lovely to see the show dogs in full coats but, in reality, most of these have many hours of work spent on them that is just not possible with a pet in a busy household, so a compromise needs to be made. The trim you choose for your dog needs to reflect the lifestyle it is leading to keep it comfortable, and also the amount of time you have to dedicate to the coat type of the dog.

I am not alone in finding that one of the most difficult coats for my clients to keep is anything that is crossed with a wool coat, for example a Poodle. A single Poodle coat is much easier to groom out as it does not have the thick dense undercoat of the crosses. The one Poodle cross that is easier to keep is the Poodle/Bichon, or Poochon, as both breeds have a wool coat so there is no dense undercoat. One thing to consider when choosing a breed of dog is, do the breeds you are interested suit your lifestyle? Would a Newfoundland really still feel welcome in a few months when it is an adult in a tiny flat and gets wet after being walked? Is a little

OPPOSITE: Who could not love this little boy? Just make sure he gets used to being groomed as early as possible.

Yorkshire Terrier suitable for a rough and tumble home with young children?

By now, you should also have a little insight into checking your dog's health and can pick up potentially problematic symptoms that, if left, may not be able to be cured. All this just by grooming your dog. If, in the end, you decide to still go to your regular groomer for styling, they will really appreciate that your dog will be clean and mat free, as groomers get very frustrated when they want to please a client with a nice trim but it is impossible because of the condition of the coat. Some of the dogs that come into groomers are really in a terrible state and tears are shed more often than they should be by staff. Grooming is not particularly easy, sometimes, mainly due to the behaviour of the dogs that have never been taught to be groomed or trained in basic obedience. If you are grooming your own dog, you will be in total control of rectifying this problem over time with a little patience, guidance and coaxing.

During the Covid pandemic lockdown, many owners started to try to groom their own dogs as there were no appointments available with a groomer. They obviously did not tackle anything complicated but, in many cases, did not do a bad job, even though it was basic and did not have the tidiness of a professional groom. I really hope that many of you will take the opportunity to get to know your dog better and reduce the frustration of dirty, matted dogs rampaging through your house for weeks if you cannot get an appointment with a groomer. Enjoy working with your precious friend and I hope you have many fruitful hours taking pride in your well-groomed dog, especially when the day comes when you are stopped in the street and asked where you get your dog groomed.

Happy grooming!

Index

First published in 2024 by
The Crowood Press Ltd
Ramsbury, Marlborough
Wiltshire SN8 2HR

enquiries@crowood.com
www.crowood.com

British Library Cataloguing-in-Publication Data
A catalogue record for this book is available from the British Library.

ISBN 978 0 7198 4307 5

Cover design by Blue Sunflower Creative

Acknowledgements
I would like to thank the following people who have assisted me with the formation of this production:
Christine McNee; Stewart Murphy; Carol Johnston; Georgina Ramsay; Mirjam Coert; Mary Danks; the staff of Techngroom, Carluke; the students of Scotgroom, Carluke.

Typeset by Simon and Sons

Printed and bound in India by Parksons Graphics Pvt. Ltd.